WHERE THERE'S AN INHERITANCE...

STORIES FROM INSIDE THE WORLD OF TWO WILLS LAWYERS

April 2010

WHERE THERE'S AN INHERITANCE…

WHERE THERE'S AN INHERITANCE...

STORIES FROM INSIDE
THE WORLD OF TWO
WILLS LAWYERS

BY BARRY M. FISH
& LES KOTZER

Continental Atlantic Publications Inc.

ISBN 978-0-9683513-9-0

American Inquiries can be made to the following address:
C/O Continental Atlantic Publications Inc.
4200 Wisconsin Avenue N.W.
P.M.B. # 106-229
Washington, D.C. 20016-2143

All other inquiries can be made to the following address:
C/O Continental Atlantic Publications Inc.
7951 Yonge Street
Thornhill, Ontario
Canada L3T2C4

Telephone Toll-Free (U.S. and Canada) 1-877-439-3999

Websites: www.familyfight.com
www.thefamilywar.com
www.aninheritance.com

The discussion in this book should not be considered legal or financial advice. Legal and financial advice can only be obtained from a professional in your jurisdiction. Please consult your own professional advisor with respect to any steps you wish to carry out as a result of reading this book. The laws governing the various topics discussed in this book will vary depending on the jurisdiction.

Printed and bound in Canada.

ABOUT THE AUTHORS

Barry M. Fish graduated from McGill University in the late 1960's with both civil law and common law degrees. He is the senior partner in his law firm, Fish & Associates, which he established in 1973. He is a member of the Society of Trust and Estate Practitioners and has a lengthy experience in the field of estate disputes. Barry is a co- author of The Family Fight…Planning to Avoid it, and The Family War…Winning the Inheritance Battle. He is a frequent radio and television guest and contributor to various newspapers and magazines. He was host of the "Protect Yourself" radio show and a frequent guest on the Money Line television show. He is married and has two children and two grandchildren. His firm's website is www.familyfight.com. Barry can be reached at bfish@fishlaw.ca.

Les Kotzer, a wills and estates lawyer since 1989, focuses his practice on avoiding and resolving inheritance disputes. He graduated law school on the Dean's List. He is a member of the Society of Trust and Estate Practitioners and is co-author of The Family Fight…Planning to Avoid it, and The Family War…Winning the Inheritance Battle.

Les is also a regular guest on television and radio shows across North America. He has appeared on CNN and Fox News. He has also been featured in publications across North America including Time Magazine, Newsweek, The Wall Street Journal, The National Post, and The New York Times. His website is www.leskotzer.com.

Les is also a professional songwriter. He has written the lyrics for the songs on the CD entitled, "A Family United, A Family Divided." Three of his songs, "These are our Heroes," "You Made a Difference," and "Photos in a Drawer," can be heard on various radio stations. He has a second website devoted to his songs, www.songwritinglawyer.com. Les can be reached at leskotzer@familyfight.com.

ACKNOWLEDGEMENTS

Even when a book is written by co-authors, the act of writing is a very lonely experience. Time swallows the minutes and the hours. The computer screen seems to be the only landscape. The comfort is that we are not really alone. Those who supported us in so many ways during the writing of this book are the staff at our office, being Benedetta, Robyn, and Risa. We also thank our true friends, Louis Manne and Wendy Watson, who gave us their help and support. Those who inspired us are our families, and to them we devote the remaining words of this acknowledgment:

BARRY M. FISH

At the time of this first printing, my mother is just turning 91 and still holding her head high as a Gold Life Master in bridge. I wrote about her when The Family War was just about to be printed and I am happy to say that in the several years that have passed since then, Mom is still sharp as a tack. She loves to tell me when she placed first with some partner at her bridge club, and I love to hear it.

My wife Pearl has been an excellent support for me. She has been a patient wife on those long days when I came home late for supper because Les and I were working on this book.
My biggest fans are my children, Joanna and Adrian. I hope to have two new fans, in my two granddaughters, Nadia and Tamara.

When I wrote acknowledgements for The Family War, I mentioned these words about my late father, Abe, and they are worth repeating here:
"The words in this book will never pass before his eyes, but it is in the words of this book that his inspiration will live."

LES KOTZER

The inspiration from my late mother, Rose, is part of my life. Not a day goes by that I don't think of her. I have always aspired to conduct myself the way I know she expected of me. My late grandfather Sam, my late grandmother Bessie, and my late auntie Sarah gave me all of their love and I miss them very much. My father, Jack, is not just my father, but a best friend. I cherish every day we have together. I owe so much to him. My brother, Joel, is everything a brother can be, and the very definition of what a brother should be. My wife Miriam is a beautiful person inside and out. She is my strength. I love her dearly. Suzie and Michelle, I am so proud of both of you. You are my treasures.

My family means everything to me.

<u>DEDICATION</u>

For:
Miriam, Suzie, and Michelle

Pearl, Joanna, Adrian, Nadia, and Baby Tamara

"It is pretty hard to tell what does bring happiness; poverty and wealth have both failed."

Kin Hubbard

TABLE OF CONTENTS

INTRODUCTION

Welcome to our world.

We are both wills lawyers. When we were in law school, we had no idea where our roads would lead after graduation. Some lawyers are involved in real estate law, criminal law, bankruptcy law, or in one of many other areas of law. The one certainty that was common to both of us was that neither of us imagined becoming wills and estates lawyers. However, after our many years of doing this for a living, neither of us would give up what we do.We want to introduce you to a book of stories which is probably unlike anything you have ever read before. We have consistently found that death and inheritance unleash a vast range of emotions which embrace bitter mean-spiritedness on one end of the spectrum, and the deepest imaginable wellsprings of goodwill and love on the other.

The inheritance-related stories you will read are based on our years in the field of wills and estates. Our personal experiences have been varied. We have met many individuals in many walks of life who have had stories to tell. We have listened intently to them. Similarly, we have lent a sensitive ear to participants at our seminars, callers on our TV and radio shows, and others in the field of wills and estates who we have met. Each person, in his or her own way, contributed to our ability to put these stories in writing.

Some of the stories in our book are based on situations where we are obliged to respect lawyer-client confidentiality. Wherever a story in our book makes reference to a client who has come to our office, we have deliberately removed all of the detail which is traceable to any of the parties involved, or their families, their businesses, or personal affairs. Nothing in our book can be traced directly or indirectly to any client of ours. We have, where necessary, varied the facts involved so that no description of what you will read in this book can lead to the identity of any person or his or her business or family. In all of our stories, what we intend to share with the reader is their emotional impact. Moments frozen in time have been preserved, and it is around these precious and fleeting experiences that the stories have been compiled. If there is one phrase to express the intention of our book, it is that the reader benefit in his or her own life by the lessons to be learned in reading these stories.

The lessons to be learned, from the pain and distress so common to family battles over inheritance, have led us to develop our own focus on how to avoid, or to at least minimize, family battles. Accordingly, we wrote The Family Fight: Planning to Avoid It, published in 2002. That book dealt with the prevention of the fight. However, we felt it was necessary to go to the next level, once the fight had begun, and to write about what people need to know about estate disputes. As a result, in 2006, we published The Family War: Winning the Inheritance Battle, which we co-authored with Jordan Atin, a certified specialist in estates and trust law. It has always been important to us that we have a vehicle to alert the public at large to some of the pitfalls that families might be able to avoid.

Finally, what we wish to share with you is this: while rules of protocol and professionalism may restrain the hand that writes and the lips that speak, nothing can restrain what lies in the hearts of those who have a message that yearns to be set free. Many of these stories have had a permanent impact on us and we believe that they will have an impact on you.

1. PILL UNDER THE TABLE

Margaret was close to turning eighty. Through the passage of so many years, she always kept a close relationship with her nieces and nephews. She called them her "babies," even when they were all in their thirties and forties.

They may have been born to Margaret's sister, but if you could have seen the way they all got along, you might have thought that they were her own children.

Very often, she would give one or other of her "babies" her car keys. Margaret would sometimes wake up to hear a couple of them washing her car. She often asked their opinion on various matters, especially when it came to her hobby of picking up antiques, something that Margaret was very good at. Her home was filled with treasures in the form of lamps and end tables, china, crystal, silver, and artwork. And Margaret's kitchen table was over a hundred years old.

When it came time for one of her "babies" to have a birthday or an anniversary, Margaret often gave them some of the smaller items from her treasures.

When Margaret was diagnosed with clogged arteries, her doctor said that it was urgent for her to have a quadruple bypass. In her case, this was a risky procedure, and her chances of surviving the surgery were less than 50-50. Her nieces and nephews visited her day and night at the hospital before her operation. At Margaret's request, her "babies" knew where her will was kept. She told them that the key to her home was in an envelope in the drawer beside her hospital bed. She said that in the event that she didn't make it through her operation, they would know that the house key was there.

Due to some complications that arose from her surgery, Margaret's stay at the hospital was three full weeks. When she was eventually released, the bad news was that the operation was a partial success and that her prognosis for a full recovery was questionable. The good news was that she was able to live at home on her own, but she had strict orders to take her medication several times a day.

Margaret intended to follow her doctor's advice to the letter. Several days after she came home, she was in the process of opening up a bottle of pills, when her hand slipped, and the contents spilled all over the table. She quickly captured her valuable pills, but one of them landed under her kitchen table.

As she bent down to pick it up, out of the corner of her eye she saw an unfamiliar yellow sticker stuck to the bottom of the table. Looking closer, she saw Jeannine's name. Jeannine was the eldest of her nieces. Margaret was puzzled. "How did that get there?" she asked herself. Then as she got up, she saw another yellow sticker underneath a shelf on her antique hutch. That one had Gretchen's name. Gretchen was her youngest niece.

This aroused her curiosity and Margaret began to go all through her home looking at lamps and bowls and platters, even the back of her large screen TV. Strips of masking tape with names written on them were stuck to the bottom of each and every stick of furniture, on every appliance, and on almost everything Margaret could lay her eyes on.

It was obvious to her that her "babies" expected her to die, and between them, they had carved up all of the contents of her home. Worse yet, her mind's eye went back to the envelope she had left in the drawer in the hospital. One of her "babies" must have taken that key while Margaret was in surgery, and then replaced it before she came to. Margaret was fuming.

Her "babies" never got to realize just how angry Margaret felt, and would never know until after Margaret died. You see, originally, Margaret was going to leave everything she owned to her "babies." Now she made a new will, and left everything she owned to charity. After she completed her new will, Margaret had one more wish. She hoped that there was life after death. She would love to be able to see the expression on the faces of each of her greedy little "babies," when they would see that she cut all of them out of her will.

2. MY UNCARING BROTHER

Sometimes, even when an estate is divided equally, there can still be other issues that can cause a falling out between siblings.

A client was in our office making her will, and when the subject of guardians for her young children came up, it seemed natural to suggest one of her siblings. She said that her only sibling was her brother. She adamantly refused to consider him. I asked her why. She then told the following story.

In 1995, her father had passed away leaving his few possessions divided equally between our client and her very wealthy brother. For her, 1995 was a horrible year. Not only had she lost her father, but as well, she had lost her home due to a bitter divorce with her husband, and suffered financial hardship from the loss of her job.

She had not asked anyone for any help with her financial situation, and her wealthy brother never offered to lend a hand. However, that alone was not what caused her to be upset.

What initiated her bitterness toward her brother can be traced to the day before the burial of her Dad. She had driven for six hours to the family home. Her brother was already there when she arrived. The entire family was grieving. Before she could even remove her jacket, her brother called her into the bedroom and closed the door. "We have to bury Dad. The funeral expenses are $7,000. I have already paid my $3,500 and I need your half now, or else Dad won't get buried."

At that time, she didn't even have $500 in the bank, let alone $3,500, and she immediately shared this fact with her brother. She knew that her brother could have paid her half of the $7,000 very easily because of his wealth and she could have paid him back over time.

Her brother was unmoved. He shrugged his shoulders. "Okay, so then Dad won't get buried." She choked back tears of frustration and said, "Let me call the funeral home." Still she had not removed her jacket. She called and arranged with the funeral home to pay her $3,500 share by credit card, but they required that any payment be dealt with in their office and not over the telephone. She left her grieving family and drove in the traffic to the funeral home and met with the person she had spoken to on the phone.

 In the business office of the funeral home, she paid her half on her credit card. This practically maxed out the credit limit on her card.

She held up her end of the deal which was mercilessly forced upon her by her brother. Her father was buried, but now she had to cope with her new debt. Every month, during the five years of struggling it took her to pay off this credit card, brought back constant memories of her brother's cold, uncaring attitude. She couldn't help but despise him for it.

Now it was clear to me why she became angry even at the thought of her brother being considered as a guardian.

3. SOMETIMES, IT'S MORE THAN THE MONEY

Most of Desmond's adult life passed under the influence of drugs and alcohol. For years, the people closest to Desmond were people his family despised. Desmond's parents demanded that he live away from the family home because too many times, there was a knock on the door or a telephone call from police. As a result, Desmond became estranged from his family. It was only when his mother died that Desmond suddenly realized the error of his ways. At that point, he earnestly and honestly sought to be rehabilitated. It was then that he took steps to make peace with his family. He met with his father and opened his heart to him. His father seemed to be receptive to Desmond. His father lived for two more years after that meeting. Over these two years, Desmond hoped that Dad had at last accepted his apologies, and had forgiven Desmond for the heartache and pain Desmond had caused him.

Several days after Dad's funeral, Desmond could hardly believe what he was reading. The lawyer who was looking after his Dad's estate showed Desmond a copy of the will Dad had left.

To Desmond's surprise, Dad's will left Desmond an equal share of the estate. He was elated that Dad seemed to be treating him the same way as his three brothers, but Desmond needed to know more.

What Desmond really wanted was to know how Dad felt about him over the two years that had passed since he had made peace with his father. The contents of Dad's will gave him a feeling of encouragement, but the answers Desmond was really looking for were to be found in his father's diaries. It was no secret that Dad wrote everything in his diaries that he felt was important. Although no one ever got to read any of Dad's diaries, the whole family knew of how

Dad wrote every day of the events of the day before, and how much his collective diaries meant to him.

Desmond knew that the diaries were in Dad's study. Getting access to them was simple. None of his brothers had a problem with Desmond taking all the time he wanted, in order to read what he wished to read.

Desmond felt suspense, as he was now about to see what Dad had written about him. He expected that some of what he was going to read would show Dad's reaction to the pain that Desmond had caused his parents. Desmond braced himself as he began to read of Dad's fishing trips, general family matters, the grandchildren, Dad's car repairs, card games, school graduations and dozens of other personal matters. Sure enough, the pages of Dad's diaries turned bitter and harsh, as they revealed how both Mom and Dad had to be medicated and to seek medical advice because of Desmond. The pages spoke of Dad missing work because of the stress caused by police visits to his home and insulting calls from angry drug dealers. The diary spoke of Mom's sleepless nights, worried about her son. Page after page revealed Dad's pain and heartbreak, explicitly blaming Desmond. At the same time, Desmond could see nothing but praise and pride in these pages, when the subject turned to Desmond's brothers.

Dad's pain was not lost on Desmond. Dad's message was loud and clear. But Desmond had come to these diaries for a more important reason. Desmond skipped to the last two years. These pages were the ones he yearned to read.

As he got into these pages, the ones that spoke of Dad's last two years, Desmond felt relief as there was no further reference to the pain he had caused his family. But as he turned page after page, his heart began to sink, looking for some reference, any reference, to his own name. But not one word on any of these pages was written about Desmond. As Desmond turned the last page of Dad's last diary, he knew in his broken heart that Dad had become numb to him and that Dad had never really forgiven him. Now Desmond knew that the warmth he felt from reading Dad's will was really an illusion.

The only closure for Desmond was that Dad had slammed the door shut on anything more that Desmond could do as a son.

Desmond had his inheritance, but he would have given all of it back if only he knew that Dad had a place in his heart for him when he died. To Desmond, this meant that even though he was in his father's will, he was not necessarily in his father's heart.

4. A BIGOTED BROTHER

Shortly after Celia started to date Graham, she met his brother Kirk at a family gathering. Within an hour of meeting Celia for the first time, Kirk told her that she was not the right kind of person for Graham and that if she had any thoughts about getting serious about Graham, she better know that his family would never accept her. Kirk made it clear that he did not like "her people."

Graham knew that his brother loathed Celia and everything about her, but he loved Celia and she became his common-law wife.

Both Graham and Celia ignored Kirk and thought that he was out of their lives. From that point on, and for the rest of Graham's life, there was a cold silence between the two brothers. After five years of living with Celia, Graham passed away, leaving a will which gave his entire estate to his common-law wife, Celia.

Several months after Graham died, Celia was astonished when she received a letter from Kirk's lawyer, claiming Kirk's entitlement to the entire estate that his brother, Graham, had left. Celia immediately showed this shocking letter to her lawyer.

When Celia's lawyer sent a copy of Graham's will to Kirk's lawyer, Celia expected this to put an end to Kirk's unwarranted intrusion into her life.

The fact that Graham had left everything to Celia in his will meant nothing to Kirk. In his attack on Celia, Kirk claimed that Graham constantly complained to him about his relationship with Celia. Kirk went on to claim that she manipulated Graham, that she had been physically violent to him, that she dominated him, and that Graham had confided in Kirk that he was going to break up with Celia.

Kirk went on to accuse Celia of exercising undue influence upon Graham to take advantage of his submissive character. The foundation of Kirk's case was that Graham's will was null and void because Graham signed that will under Celia's threats to do violence to him if he didn't give her everything.

This case quickly descended into a fight that was so bitter that words fail to adequately describe it.

Celia decided that she would fight Kirk, holding nothing back.

She countered that Kirk was a racist, a bigot, a mean-spirited man who was so spurned by women through his life that he became a woman-hater. She went on to speak of his hatred of people of Celia's race and religion, and it was this hatred that led Kirk to manufacture a fictitious attack totally at odds with the reality of her loving relationship with Graham.

Kirk put Celia to the test. His legal argument was that whatever Celia stated consisted of nothing more than bald accusations and lies. Kirk said that Graham would never go against the wishes of their parents to keep everything in their family, and that the will that Celia was attempting to uphold, was exactly opposite to what Graham strongly believed in.

Celia and her lawyer felt that enough was enough. Celia prepared a binder of birthday cards, anniversary cards, picture albums, affidavits from close friends, all showing how Celia and Graham never lost the love and infatuation that brought them together. There were highly personal notes from Graham to her: "you are a godsend....you are the best thing that ever happened to me....I will love you forever." There were dozens of love notes from Graham to her. All of this formed part of the binder. What the binder also contained was a letter from Kirk accusing his brother of bringing filth into the family. Kirk had signed another letter saying that he was disgusted that Graham would even associate with anyone of Celia's race.

Celia's lawyer was experienced enough to know that if Kirk kept on with this style of legal proceeding, Kirk would pay an overwhelming cost penalty. The evidence of Kirk's venom was abundant, but there was not a shred of evidence to support Kirk's accusations of Celia's violence and manipulation. Celia's lawyer was very familiar with a legal system that frowned upon anyone who wasted the court's time and abused the court process, with a case cast in exaggerative language but completely devoid of merit.

Kirk's lawyer also understood. Kirk may have been blinded by his hatred and bigotry, but his lawyer was well aware of the crushing cost burden under which Kirk's case would be buried if it went any further.

Kirk agreed to withdraw his case and to bow out of the affairs of his brother's estate.

Celia was gracious in victory. She packaged up all of Graham's family heirlooms that were in her house and paid for their delivery to Kirk's home. She also donated $10,000 in the name of Graham's deceased parents to a local charity, in order to pay tribute to them, even though she never knew them. She then forever dismissed Kirk and his bigotry from her life.

5. IT CAUSED MY SECOND DIVORCE

Anne called us on a radio show to speak of her divorce. We politely explained to her that this show was about wills and estates, and that the subject of divorce was not a topic which would be covered. But Anne promised that her story was going to fit in with our show. This is Anne's story.

She had been married and had two teenage sons when her husband divorced her. She was an executive working for a bank, and continued to have a decent lifestyle. Her boys were old enough to decide which parent they wanted to live with and they chose her. Anne was very close to her sons. After about a year of being single, she met Andrew and fell in love with him. He had also been divorced and had a ten-year-old daughter. They decided before long to move in together. While Anne came through her divorce with substantial assets and a very good income, Andrew was left almost insolvent after his divorce. However, when he married Anne, his financial problems were resolved. Anne felt that as husband and wife, they should work on their financial planning together, and it was at that point that the subject of making their wills came up.

It was decided that they would both use the same lawyer and they felt that meeting with their lawyer to work out their thoughts would be the most efficient way of getting this done.

At the meeting which Anne arranged with the lawyer, he started off by asking what she and Andrew had in mind. In everyday language, this is roughly what she and Andrew had to say:

Anne: "Well, I want to be fair to Andrew and also to my boys, so I think we should set up my will so that he will inherit one-half of my estate and my boys will get the other half."

Andrew: "What do you mean, I only get half? I thought you were going to leave me everything! I'm your husband!"

Anne: "Why would I leave you everything? I have two boys to protect."

Andrew: "Don't worry, whatever you leave me, I will leave to your sons when I die. I'll even put it in my will right now."

At that point, Anne asked the lawyer, "If I die before Andrew, and we make wills the way Andrew wants us to, is it possible for Andrew to change his will afterward?" The lawyer answered that anyone can change his or her will as long as he or she is mentally capable.

She then turned to Andrew and said, "So, I have no guarantee that you won't change your will and cut my boys out if I die before you do."

Andrew: "I am giving you my word. Don't you trust me?"

Anne: "I trust you Andrew, but I have my two boys to protect."

At that point Andrew flew into a rage, tore up all of Anne's working papers and notes which were on the table, and swore at Anne, insulting her in front of the lawyer. He slammed the door and left the building.

Anne next saw Andrew sitting in her car. She then found herself driving home with a foul-mouthed man beside her, who was showing her a side of himself that she had never seen or even imagined him to be capable of.

Without a word to Andrew, she opened the door to the house, picked up the telephone, and called the lawyer who she had used for her first divorce.

6. MOM'S LEGACY OF LOVE

As lawyers retained to look after estates, we normally meet with the executors. We don't usually meet with an entire family. However, there is one family who left such a warm impression on us that we could not do justice to this book without including their touching story.

Elizabeth died, leaving six adult children surviving her. Her will named two of them as executors, but all six children came to our office together, because their executor siblings insisted that all of them be there. They described how their mother was left a widow, shortly after the birth of the last child. Financially, life was a struggle for all of them, but they explained how Mom's spirit allowed them to surmount the worst of times together.

They lived in the small home their father left, but it was almost totally mortgaged. Mom had good friends to help her with raising the children, and as a result, she was able to get an extra job during weekday evenings. She taught the children how to look for coupons in newspapers and flyers. She taught them how to shop using the coupons, and how to look for store specials.

She taught them how to be organized and also taught them the importance of looking out for one another. Whether it was a trip to the library, or sharing hand-me-downs, the children knew how to get the most mileage out of what they had. Every one of her children remembered the times when their mother confessed that she was sorry that she could not give them everything that their schoolmates had.

They all remembered how strong their mother looked even after the long hours of work that never seemed to end. They said that their mother was beautiful in her own way, where you could look beyond her weather-beaten appearance to actually feel her glow. So when Mom apologized for what she could not give them, they told her that what they got from her was priceless. What she gave them was far more valuable than the fancy clothes worn by their friends.

The family somehow managed through many difficult years. Now, four of the children were successful professionals, having graduated from universities. Two of them were not so fortunate, and they never escaped from hard times. One of the two suffered through a bad divorce that had left her almost penniless. The other had a business, but there were reversals of fortune that almost wiped him out financially.

Over the many lean years, their mother, Elizabeth, had constantly worked and saved what she could. Now, the little house she struggled so hard to keep, was worth close to half a million dollars and there was no longer a mortgage on it. Her will left everything she owned equally to her six children.

What so impressed us was the attitude of Elizabeth's children. All four of the successful ones sitting at our boardroom table said that all they cared about was that their less fortunate brother and sister be looked after. They said that whatever it takes, they must be helped. And they did not stop with these kind words. All four of them unanimously instructed us then and there that we were to do all the paperwork necessary in order to turn over Elizabeth's entire estate to their two siblings who needed it most.

We have rarely seen such closeness in a family. The brother and the sister, who had fallen upon their own hard times, had no idea that this was coming. They had tears in their eyes. They did not know what to say. One of the four others said it all for them, "We know you two would have done the same for us if the situation were reversed. Mom raised us to be there for each other and that will never change. Mom taught us the real meaning of love and the importance of family. That was her gift to all of us."

Without a doubt, Elizabeth would have been proud.

7. THE PIANO

Deborah was a music major at a local university. For as long as she could remember, her grandfather's Heintzman piano was a part of her family. Dad took the piano into their home after Grandpa passed away.

She spent hours upon hours every week practicing on it. Everyone knew it was hers, except that Dad never formally gave it to her. That didn't matter, somehow, until Dad passed away.

Dad died a widower, leaving his five adult children. Dad was of the old school. He never spoke of what he had, or of things like a will. Deborah never pressed him on it because she did not want to feel like she had her hands in his pockets and did not want to look greedy. As well, she did not want to offend him. She felt that Dad would look after all of his children in his own way. She also felt that her brothers and sisters all knew that Dad wanted her to have the piano.

When Dad passed away, all five children mourned his passing together, and a fight was the furthest thing from their minds. After respecting his passing, the children began to look around for his will. For over two weeks they looked everywhere. Scraps of information came to them almost accidentally, such as the legal papers about Dad's house, some scattered banking information, reference to a safety deposit box, and even its key. At that point Robert, one of her brothers, suggested that they all go together to the safety deposit box, to see if a will was in it. If there was no will in the safety deposit box, they all agreed that they would appoint Robert as administrator of the estate through Court.

With this arrangement in place, they retained a lawyer and all of them went to the bank and opened the safety deposit box. There were valuable stocks and bonds in there but no will. As agreed among them, the lawyer applied to Court and Robert became the estate administrator after months of legal paperwork.

Almost immediately after Robert's Court appointment, conflict began to emerge among the siblings. The conflict almost always took the same form. One sibling would refer to Dad's promise to give him this and another sibling would refer to Dad's promise to give her that. Every time Robert's answer was, "Sorry, but there's no will and everything will be sold and the money divided equally." Deborah always got along with Robert, and was shocked when he rejected her reminder that "everyone knows that Dad wanted me to have the piano."

After all, since Grandpa's time, no one else in the family took piano lessons, let alone expressed an interest in music. But they all knew that Deborah was a music major at the university and was on that piano almost every day.

Robert arranged for an appraiser to evaluate all of the furniture and personal effects in Dad's house. It was clear that when the appraiser completed his report to Robert, that report would include a value for the piano. Robert made it clear that the piano was going to be treated exactly the same way as everything else in the house.

Deborah told Robert that if he would not give her the piano, then she would buy it from the estate. She told Robert that this piano was in the family for over two generations and it would break her heart for a stranger to have it.

She felt suspense and anxiety the day when the appraiser had to report to Robert on the price of the Heintzman. She actually felt nervous speaking to her own brother, asking him for the price. It was high, much higher than she expected, but she felt she could raise the money in about six months. She asked him if she could pay over time. Robert said, "I'll give you exactly three months to the day to come up with the money, or it will be sold."

She had never heard her brother talk to her this way. It was as if she were speaking to some hard businessman, not her brother. But he was in a position of power, as estate administrator, and there was nothing she could do.

To Deborah, it seemed almost impossible to raise the cash so quickly. She asked one of her sisters to help her, and her sister agreed to borrow the money for her. Deborah's sister was astonished that her brother could behave so cold-heartedly.

As Robert's deadline approached, Deborah was ready. She showed up at Robert's office with the money. When they sat down, he looked at her, then down at the envelope that had her bank draft in it, without opening it. "What's wrong?" she asked.

Robert replied, "I sold it yesterday for thousands more than you offered, and I knew there was no way that you could come up with that kind of money. It's already gone." He said, "Sorry, but I suddenly got an offer that was very generous." He described this offer as a "one time take it or leave it" offer. His duties to the estate meant that he had to sell what he could for the highest price possible.

Deborah was devastated that her brother could betray her like this.

Deborah hired a lawyer to sue Robert and the estate, for his breach of the contract to sell her that piano for the agreed price. She was not bluffing. She did sue.

In the end, Robert found himself offering the buyer of the piano thousands more than the price that it was sold for, in order to fulfill a legal obligation to sell his sister a Heintzman piano of that quality. When that buyer refused to give up the piano, Robert had to try to find another one of equal quality and still could not find one. Finally, Deborah settled with Robert. To avoid a court battle, he agreed to pay her damages of twice the amount that she originally offered to pay him for that Heintzman.

Robert found no sympathy from any of his siblings who were sharing in the estate. They said that he had only himself to blame and that power trips did not belong in their family. In the end, Robert not only paid the damages to Deborah personally, from his own pocket, but he also lost the respect of all of his siblings. As for Deborah, she bought another Heintzman. She played the same music, but never again did her fingers tap the keys she had grown up with.

8. JUST WHEN WE THOUGHT WE'D SEEN IT ALL

Sometimes we begin to think that we have seen it all, only to be astonished by the lengths a person might be driven to by his or her fury. We will now share two expressions of outrage with you. The point of these two stories has nothing to do with whether the fury of the people involved is justified or not. The point is simply to demonstrate how far a person may go to express his or her anger, and to demonstrate very clearly that we have definitely "not seen it all."

In the first story, we acted for two brothers who were the executors of the estate of their late mother. The estate was to be divided equally, one third to each of them and one third to their sister, Lana.

Serious disagreements had arisen between Lana and themselves. Lana was challenging every decision they had made as executors. The brothers wished to arrange a meeting with us in order to discuss the estate, which was quickly becoming problematic. The meeting was scheduled as they had requested.

A day or so prior to our meeting, a knapsack was delivered to our office. It came from Lana. It was sealed with tape. Attached to the knapsack was a handwritten note which stated that the contents were confidential, only to be opened by her eldest brother.

Since both brothers were scheduled to be at our office for this meeting, they asked that we hold the knapsack for them until we met.

At the beginning of our meeting with them, we placed the knapsack on the boardroom table. The elder brother immediately opened it.

First to spill onto the table were shredded remnants of fifteen or twenty sheets of paper. Each appeared to have been ripped into three, four, or five pieces. Not one of those sheets was intact. The elder brother appeared to be in shock, as he began to recognize what these ripped up papers actually were. He exclaimed to his brother, "These were the letters you and I wrote to Mom and Dad when we were kids in camp! They said that they would never part with them! How did Lana get her hands on these? Did she break into Mom's house? How could she stoop so low?"

Aside from the torn up letters were many photographs of the two brothers at various ages. Some of them were baby pictures defaced with filthy language printed over them. Others were of the two brothers with their bodies intact but their faces were cut out. Others were ripped in half. Still other photographs of the brothers had moustaches and animal tails and swear words written on them with an ink marker. On one photograph, the word "thieves" was scribbled.

The last item pulled from that knapsack was a partially destroyed porcelain figurine. It no longer resembled whatever it must have originally looked like. The elder brother was clearly shaken up as he told us that his mother bought that figurine in Italy. He said that she bought it because it represented her family. He said that this figurine originally contained figures of two adults and three children holding hands. Apparently that was a piece that his mother was proud to show at Christmas and other family gatherings. He said, "Mom always told us that the three figurine children represented us." Now the figurine was in pieces. Lana had preserved the two severed heads though, which rolled aimlessly on the boardroom table as the elder brother moved the knapsack.

Lana had broken off two of the three heads of the children in that figurine, and that is how the figurine was stuffed into the knapsack.

There was no question that this had its intended effect on the two brothers. They looked horrified at the message that their sister was sending them. It was clear from what the two brothers said that there was no way to salvage the relationship with their sister. They ended their comments with a statement to the effect that the only thing they were trying to accomplish was an equal distribution of Mom's estate. They were astounded that their sister had descended to depths that were disgraceful and which were totally disrespectful to their parents. As the brothers began to clean up the clutter on the table, the older brother said, "It is unforgivable to turn our memories into garbage," and his brother said, "I'll never forgive Lana either."

The second story shows yet another display of fury.

An estate can seem to be running smoothly from the lawyer's point of view. However, in reality, what may not be apparent to the lawyer might be vicious fights between heirs to the estate over the personal effects and household items of the deceased. There are times when the lawyer is the last to be informed about a fight of this nature, and there are times when the lawyer has no involvement at all.

We represented Karen, the executor of her mother's estate. At the outset, this estate did not appear to be problematic.

We were taken by surprise one afternoon, returning from lunch, when a woman appeared in our parking lot. She identified herself as Karen's sister and said that she was one of the heirs in her mother's estate. She had a message for Karen: "Karen will know all about the antique crystal vase. I am the one who bought it for Mom." She went on to say that Karen was ignoring the fact that she bought the vase as a gift for her mother for her 75th birthday, and now that her mother had passed away, she felt it was hers to keep.

She began to raise her voice as she told us how Karen was threatening her with a lawsuit if she did not give the vase back to the estate. Once we mentioned to her, politely, that she should speak to Karen about buying it back from her mother's estate, the woman's anger seemed to grow with almost every breath she took. There seemed to be no room to get a word in to respond to her, no way to calm her down. Her face had turned red and she was shaking with anger as she turned to open her car door. She reached into the front seat and held the crystal vase over her head. She shrieked at us, "IF I CAN'T HAVE THE VASE, THEN NO ONE CAN!!!" With those words, she shattered the vase on the pavement of the parking lot, jumped into her car, and took off.

Needless to say, we were stunned. We could not believe our eyes.

9. THE AFTERMATH OF A FAMILY DISPUTE

When we speak of hostility between family members, whether it is over a bank account or a crystal vase, there is an aftermath. The next story illustrates what this aftermath can feel like.

After his father died, Bob fought over the family business with his cousin Fred, who also worked in the business. What each of them took away from the fight was bitterness. Each of them came face-to-face with this bitterness when both 'were invited to the same wedding, and both were seated at the same table. Lavish courses of soup, salad, and dinner, and indescribably beautiful flowers did nothing to soothe the awkwardness Bob felt in trying to avoid looking at Fred.

This bitterness had spread to Bob's wife, who also had to do everything in her power to avoid looking at Fred. Other relatives, who were seated at Bob and Fred's table, knew nothing of their fight. They couldn't understand the coldness between these brothers as they unwittingly tried to engage both Bob and Fred in conversation.

Bob, who told us this story, said that he had no words to express how upset he felt whenever he saw Fred whispering in the ear of the person sitting beside him. Was Fred talking about him? Was Fred whispering his side of the story? Was Fred trying to ruin Bob's reputation? Or, was Fred just talking about what he read in today's newspaper? Bob said that the suspense was almost unbearable, waiting for the moment when Fred might start blaming him in front of everyone at the table. Or, would Fred hold his tongue?

"You don't know what it is like to kick your wife under the table to make sure that she won't trigger something with an off-the-cuff comment.

You don't know how it feels to look at every person at the table as a buffer between you and the person you fought with.

You don't know how nervous you might get meeting your enemy while the two of you are alone in the washroom. There is a stress that words can't describe. You take special precautions to prevent being in the same place as he is."

Bob said that when he fought with Fred, he never bargained for any of this. He thought he would never see Fred again for the rest of his life. He also never bargained for a fast exit from a beautiful wedding that to him was a night of tension, anxiety, and stress.

10. A MOTHER'S HEART

Cynthia had very little time left. Her doctor had diagnosed her with a terminal illness. He told Cynthia that she had better get her affairs in order.

That led to her appointment with me.

In the course of the discussion between the two of us, Cynthia told me that she had at most a month left to live, and she had to talk to me about her heaviest burden. I was surprised to hear that the one thing weighing more heavily on her mind than her illness was the deteriorated relationship between her son and daughter. They were her only two children. She had raised them with all of her love. They were always so close to one another and they meant everything to Cynthia. "But now," she said, "you'd think my kids were strangers." She told me that she had shed too many tears over this. She was so upset that she could no longer get a good night's sleep.

Cynthia went on to explain that her son's wife and her daughter's husband were controlling and manipulative people. Unfortunately, over time, Cynthia said that their negative influences caused each of her two children to become brainwashed to the point that they became competitive with one another. They mistrusted one another. A general animosity formed between her two children. They became jealous of one another and Cynthia felt that a divisive wall between the two of them left her children cold and distant from each other.

Cynthia began to cry as she described how her children hardly ever spoke to one another, and that they had stopped going to family gatherings. She said that after she was gone, the situation would become worse, and she told me that she could not pass away without trying to resolve this family crisis.

Cynthia knew that if she named her children as the executors in her will, they would find reasons to fight with one another. She could not name one without the other. What she wanted was to name me as her sole executor.

Having heard Cynthia's deepest fears and the way she expressed herself to me, I could tell that she was an intelligent and organized person. She explained every aspect of her financial situation, and provided me with a list of every important person to contact about her affairs.

I felt sympathetic to what she was trying to achieve, and therefore told her that it would be my privilege to act as her executor after she had passed away.

However, I told her that I still had misgivings about how the hostility between her two children would be resolved.

She smiled sadly, and said that when she would return to my office next week to sign her will, she would show me what she had in mind.

The next week, she signed her will. After she signed it, Cynthia handed me a large sealed brown envelope. Her instructions as to what would happen after her funeral were simple:

I was to arrange an appointment with both of her children to meet with me. She specified that both children must be together at that meeting with me.

Secondly, this meeting had to be without either of their spouses, and the two children had to be sitting in two chairs side by side, not at opposite sides of the table.

Thirdly, I must open the sealed envelope in their presence, and must go over the entire contents with them.

Only after these three steps were completed, was I authorized to discuss the distribution of her estate.

That meeting was the last I ever had with Cynthia.

Her son called me about 48 hours after her funeral, to ask me about her will. I told him that his mother had left me instructions, and that I would be calling his sister to meet with us for the next step in dealing with the estate. He seemed to be disappointed to hear that he would be in a meeting with his sister. However, I gathered that he resigned himself to going through the motions he had to go through in order to get his share of the estate.

About a week later, I met with Cynthia's two children. It was easy to see what Cynthia had meant, in describing the coldness and the distance between the two of them. Each of them seemed to search for a focal point in the room which would ensure that their gazes never met. I told them that it was one of their mother's last wishes that they be seated side by side. This definitely did not please them, but they respected their mother's wishes. They sat on one side of the boardroom table and I sat opposite them.

Before touching my estate file, I placed the brown sealed envelope on the table.

I was personally curious as to what it was that I was opening up. The envelope was very heavy. I felt two sets of eyes watching my every move as I carefully slit one end of this sealed envelope. I shook out a dark brown photo album. On its front cover, in large white marker, were the words, "For my children, who are all that I have."

My instructions were to go over with both children, what the envelope contained. Following these instructions as logically as I could, I turned the album around so that they could see it, and I opened it to the first page. Now I was the one who watched, as their eyes took in the pictures in that album.

Their eyes were riveted on pictures and on Cynthia's writing in pen beside many of those pictures. They were staring at the first page, and the brother looked at his sister before turning it, and she nodded and then they were at the second opened page. Now their gazes were intent, dwelling on the pictures and the writings. It seemed like minutes were passing before the sister looked at her brother and he nodded and the page was turned. Now I could see her eyes moisten. I leaned over to better see what the two of them were looking at, and then went around the table to their side. There was a black-and-white picture of a baby girl, and a little boy kissing her on the cheek. The words "my precious treasures" were written beside it.

I excused myself for a few minutes, leaving the two of them to continue with the photo album. When I returned, they both had tears in their eyes. They showed me about a dozen pictures, which they had removed from the album and placed on the boardroom table. One was of the daughter, with her first name written on a piece of paper pinned to her sweater. She could not have been more than six years old, from the look of it. Her brother was holding her hand. At that point her brother said to me, "This was her first day in school and Mom wanted me to take her to school. I held her hand all the way." There were several more pictures of the children at birthday parties, feeding a small deer in a zoo, and still they were turning pages.

Suddenly, both of them reached to pull out a picture of themselves as teenagers, playing Frisbee on a beach. Cynthia's son said, "That was the best summer we ever had." Cynthia's daughter said that she never laughed so hard in her life as she did that summer.

Mom had snapped a picture at her son's university graduation, and now it was the sister who was kissing her brother on the cheek in that picture.

Cynthia's daughter then turned to her brother with tears in her eyes, her voice shaking, "We lost Mommy. She's gone. How could we have hurt her? What have we done?" Her brother was wiping away his tears too, and said, "We lost her, but we can't lose each other." With that, the two of them hugged.

This was getting very emotional. There was one more thing for me to do. I pulled out a letter from the envelope, and placed it in front of them. It was a handwritten letter from Mom.

The letter spoke of how, when they were very young, they would snuggle up with Mom when she would read the stories that were special to them. The letter went on to describe how each of them always looked out for one another. He protected his sister from bullies and watched out for her in the schoolyard. When she went out on a date, he was always worried about the type of boy she was going out with. She made sure he got all of his schoolwork when he was sick at home with mononucleosis. Every day, she would go to his teacher to get his work.

The letter went on to remind each of them of all that they had been to each other. Mom's letter went on to tell them how she wanted them to always treasure one another the way she treasured them.

At the end of this letter were Mom's final words: "I want both of you to always be close to one another, and remember, I'll be watching you."

After they read this letter, Cynthia's two children were so emotional that neither of them wanted to hear anything about the will, the estate, or business. They wanted an appointment in a couple of weeks to deal with all of that. For now, all they wanted was to leave together with the photo album and Mom's letter, and that is how they left.

There is a postscript to this story. I met with them about ten days later. It was almost as if I was speaking to two entirely different people. Their body language, the warmth in the way they spoke to one another, even their expressions bore no resemblance to the cold and distant brother and sister I had met less than two weeks earlier.

As the two of them were signing documents, the sister smiled at me. "Mom knew who we really were," she said, and from the way she said these words, and in the way she smiled, for just a brief second, I saw Cynthia in her.

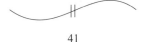

11. WAS IT REALLY WORTH IT?

Two cousins were fighting a serious battle over the estate left by their aunt. There was a lot at stake, and fortunately, both sides to the case were represented by lawyers with common sense, and they were able to come to a settlement of the financial issues without having to go to court. However, in order to complete the settlement, the jewellery, art, and household items in their aunt's estate had to be distributed. This meant that the two cousins and their lawyers had to meet in the aunt's home to work out who would get which item.

There were fights over almost everything. When it was agreed that the glassware would be divided equally, each of the two cousins wanted to take all of the tall glasses, leaving the short glasses to the other cousin. Neither of them wanted to break up any sets of glassware and it took the innovation of the lawyers to have one of the cousins agree to take the short glasses in return for the first pick over some silverware.

The cousins were very hostile to each other and the only reason that they were able to finalize their settlement at all, was because they knew that a failure to settle this distribution would be so costly that they would be paying out more in lawyer's fees and court costs than the items in their aunt's home were worth.

It took hours of arguing, and the insults and offensive remarks made the settlement process hard to endure. Finally, the distribution was agreed upon. One cousin packed up the items in a van that was in the driveway, leaving the other cousin to keep what was left in her aunt's home.

The cousin who kept the items which were left, including the tall glassware, also received her aunt's home, as part of the overall settlement.

It seemed that this cousin was finally going to find peace after all of that fighting. She may have found her peace, but a month after the settlement was concluded the house was broken into and a thief made off with almost every single item of value that she had fought so hard to keep.

12. HE'S A WAITER

Looking out of the office window, I saw a very expensive sports car pulling into a parking space in our parking lot. A well-dressed couple got out. They appeared to be in their fifties, and had come for their appointment to give me instructions to make their wills.

I could not help noticing the extraordinary quality of the watches each of them was wearing. The wife was wearing a lot of jewellery. Particularly noticeable was her diamond tennis bracelet. It happened to catch the light, and my eyes were drawn to its gleam and sparkle. Her purse bore a logo from a well-known and very expensive Italian designer.

Our discussion began with basic information, such as their names and their home address. Their address made it clear to me that they lived in a very expensive area of the city. They made a point of telling me that they lived right next door to a well-known media personality, and beside her, lived the chief executive officer of a major corporation. I immediately formed the impression that these people were wealthy.

However, as the details of their finances began to unfold, my first impressions began to melt away. They told me that because they had used the equity in their home to secure the line of credit that they constantly drew money from, their home was so heavily mortgaged that there was hardly any equity left in it at all. They had a business but it became insolvent and they had to make arrangements with the creditors of the business. Their sports car was leased. They had dozens of credit cards, using the unused room left on one card in order to pay the minimum balance on another. The wife worked as a part-time substitute teacher. As well, she tutored some children at nights and on weekends.

It seemed that nothing in their financial situation could possibly allow them to live the lifestyle that they were displaying to the outside world. Despite all of this, the wife gave me the impression that they weren't worried about their financial situation.

When finally I was able to ask the husband what he did for a living, now that he no longer had his business, his wife, smiling, interrupted him. "Harry's a waiter," she interjected. This puzzled me. I asked Harry respectfully what kind of an establishment he was serving in, expecting that perhaps he made tips which might provide some of the money that their lifestyle was gobbling up. "No," his wife again answered for him. "He's not that kind of a waiter." She continued. "I call him a waiter because he's waiting for his inheritance."

Now Harry spoke. "My wife mocks me, but I tell her that we'll be okay. We shouldn't be worried." In a calm voice, he told me that his mother had never spent a penny of her savings. She was almost 90 and in very poor health. He was her only child. He had seen her will, which left her entire estate to him. He smiled confidently when he said this. He went on to say that after his mother passes away, his money problems will be solved forever. "So why should we lose any sleep?"

He had made his point.

I wondered, after this couple left the office, how many other "waiters" there were out there.

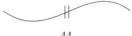

13. A SPECIAL GIFT

A caller on a radio show had heartfelt words for her recently deceased mother-in-law, whose will left her an expensive gold ring.

She said that she was very moved by the fact that she was even named as a beneficiary in her mother-in-law's will, because none of her friends and no one in her family had ever heard of a daughter-in-law being named in the will of a mother-in-law. The caller would have been surprised just to have been left a small token gift.

Inheriting this gold ring made her feel as if she were a daughter, as opposed to a daughter-in-law. It was a family heirloom, and had been passed down to her mother-in-law from previous generations. Along with the will, her mother-in-law also left a personal note. Our caller felt that this note showed what was really important to some people, and she asked if she might be allowed to read it out on the radio. She said that she loved and respected her mother-in-law, and that what she was about to read had nothing to do with money. In part, the note from the deceased spoke of how the caller treated the deceased during her lifetime. The mother-in-law's note praised her daughter-in-law for treating her the way a loving daughter is supposed to treat a mother.

"You were always there for me. You never made me feel like a burden, and whenever I needed you, you came. There were times when I never had to ask anything of you because you always offered. My son always told me that you were the one who encouraged him to spend more time with me."

We were happy that she read this out to the audience. True enough, there were no fundamental teachings or dramatic images in what she read. What she did share was a touching expression of appreciation from a mother-in- law to a daughter-in-law, for acts of kindness over a period of years. That was worth sharing with the world.

14. SOMETIMES, YOU HAVE TO CRY

We have found that over time, lawyers can become drawn into the lives of their clients. After all, clients tend to share very personal information as they seek the professional guidance of the lawyer. Many times, clients will tell their lawyers things that even their closest family members do not know. The professional relationship between lawyer and client can, therefore, become very personal.

To illustrate this point, I think of one of my clients, Quentin. In the 1970's he first crossed my path looking for assistance with a mortgage on his home so that he could put some money into his small manufacturing business. He was a former alcoholic who turned his life into a success story. He worked very hard and eventually brought a partner into his business. The business expanded, and he bought a building.

However, there were problems associated with owning this business. Customers who would not pay, suppliers who failed to deliver, employees who had to be fired, or city inspectors who criticized his building, all formed part of the pattern of his communications with me. As his business began to prosper and money began to flow, there were other problems. Ultimately, he had a bitter fight with his partner. The business was in crisis. I worked together with Quentin to get past all of this. Just when it seemed that life returned to normal, his wife left him.

Battling through another crisis in his life brought Quentin to the brink of the worst of his fears. He used me as if I were his psychologist. He thought of killing himself. I recall "talking him down" even though this is not something lawyers do for a living.

The crisis passed, and a large competitor offered to buy his little company for over two million dollars. The deal was a sweet one for him. They agreed to keep Quentin on as an executive, paying him hundreds of thousands of dollars a year plus a car and benefits.

I helped him with this buyout and it was one of the few times when I actually attended a celebration party for a client.

At the party, Quentin made a speech about those in his life who meant so much to him. When he mentioned my name, the way he did, this meant more to me than anything material he could have given me.

I was more than moved by this. At that party, he handed me a fortune cookie. My cookie had a little slip of paper. "Look forward to great fortune and a new lease on life! Lucky numbers 13, 21, 24, 26, 31, 33."

As Quentin passed his sixtieth birthday, he consistently seemed more upbeat when he called me. Now, his calls were about how he was going to loan some money to his children, and about revising his own will. Our discussion was no longer about the many problems that had plagued him throughout the earlier parts of his life.

Whenever he called, we would always find time to joke about the old days. It was time for Quentin to enjoy life.

It was on a Tuesday that Quentin's son called me at my office, telling me that he had something difficult to discuss. I thought that this was the new generation about to ask for help with a legal problem.

His son seemed hesitant to tell me what he called for. Then he blurted out, "We knew you would be hurt when we told you this, so it was hard to make this call. Dad passed away on a job site. He suddenly had a massive heart attack and died."

As Quentin's son was telling me this, my eyes fell on the piece of paper that I retrieved from the fortune cookie Quentin had given me. I had kept it on my desk all this time. (In fact, I have no plans of ever removing it from that spot).

What I can remember from the rest of that telephone call was Quentin's son asking me, "Barry, are you still there? Are you okay Barry? Are you okay? I am so sorry that I had to call you with such bad news."

I could not speak for the tears that were choking me as I was flooded with emotion. I was speechless. All I could do was to think about the legal tightropes and the rocky paths that Quentin and I walked together over the many years.

Snapping my attention back to the telephone in my hand, I managed to blurt out that I was still on the phone, and assured him that I would be there for the family. That brought to an end, the call with Quentin's son. I then found myself numbly putting on my jacket and going home. Even though it was early in the afternoon, I knew I would not be able to function the rest of the day. Quentin and I had been through a lot together - and I never got to say "goodbye."

15. MY FATHER SIGNED TWO DIFFERENT WILLS ON THE SAME DAY

After the conclusion of one of our radio shows, a man who was working at the radio station said that we hadn't heard it all until we heard the story he had to tell. This is Keith's story.

Keith was one of two sons from his late father's first marriage.

His mother passed away in the late nineties. A few years later, his father got remarried to a woman named Constance. She was a domineering and controlling person almost from the first moment she entered Keith's life. Keith looked upon Constance as the prime example of an evil stepmother.

About a year before Keith's father died, he decided to put his affairs in order. However, the process did not proceed very smoothly. From what Keith described to us, his father was under pressure from Constance, to make his will the way she wanted him to make it. Constance practically dictated to her husband, what she wanted his will to say. She insisted upon being present when he gave his instructions to the lawyer. She had read the draft of his will when it was first prepared and demanded changes for her protection. He agreed. The final draft of the will was given to Keith's father on the morning of his appointment for signing it. Constance took the final draft from her husband and read it over while in the waiting room at his lawyer's office. Even before seeing the lawyer, Constance demanded that her husband sign his will exactly as it was now written, "or else."

In order to appease his wife, Keith's father signed that will.

After the will was signed, the lawyer kept the original and gave a photocopy of it to Keith's father, who took it home that same day.

A few hours after his father came home from that appointment with his lawyer, he asked both Keith and his brother to come into his private home office.

Behind closed doors, and in the absence of Constance, Keith's father explained how he felt pressured by his wife. Then he told them all the details of the way she domineered him. He also explained how unhappy he felt with the way his will was drawn and signed. Constance was sole executor and beneficiary.

Now that father and sons could speak privately, Keith's father spoke of his true feelings. He was experiencing chest pains and wished to avoid any possibility that he would pass away with this will in place. He then explained that what he really wished was to leave his estate to Keith and his brother, and to have both boys act as executors. Unfortunately, he was fearful of an emotional blow-up with his wife. As well, he explained that he was too embarrassed at the lawyer's office to demand a redraft of the will, so he signed it as it was. He told the boys that he intended to do another will to revoke the one that the lawyer drew up, and that Constance would never get to know about the new will.

That secret meeting ended with Keith's father telling both boys that he was going to make a new will which would follow the wishes he had just explained to them. He said that if anything ever happened to him, they would be able to find this new will in the bottom drawer of his desk. He also cautioned them that if Constance ever found out about what they were talking about, she would make all of their lives miserable, so that the subject of the new will had to remain a secret just between the three of them. For the sake of peace, it was imperative that Constance think that his last will was the one done in the lawyer's office.

As it turned out, peace did prevail, until Keith's father passed away. It was at that point that the confrontation between stepsons and stepmother began.

The first and most immediate step that Keith and his brother knew they had to take was to go to their father's desk and look for the will that their father had spoken about in their secret meeting. Sure enough, they found that will, but to Keith's surprise, the will was a homemade one. Keith had expected to find a lawyer-drawn will. However, at least it was a will. The next surprise came several days after he and his brother had confronted Constance and showed her that the will she had was revoked. When the two wills were compared, Keith saw that both of them were dated on the exact same date. It was then that Keith recalled how his father had closed his office door and stayed alone after their secret meeting. Keith now realized that his father had drawn up that homemade will right after that secret meeting.

Before long, the boys were battling their stepmother. New lawyers quickly entered the fight. The lawyer who prepared the will that Constance relied upon would be a witness. Constance argued that the homemade will was a temporary one which was changed at the lawyer's office by a "proper" will. She also argued that her husband made his homemade will under pressure from the boys. Keith and his brother argued that the timing of the wills was crucial and that the homemade will revoked the earlier one done at the lawyer's office. They further argued that the homemade will was the document that reflected their father's true intentions.

Keith's father had signed two wills on the same day. Each of the wills stipulated that it revoked all previous wills. These two wills established the basis for the battle between Constance and her stepsons. Because wills are not completed with stamps showing the hour and the minute of signing, there was no way of knowing who the judge would believe if and when this case might come to court. However, the lawyer acting for Keith and his brother explained that the judge who would hear the case would rely on the best evidence of timing and that the wills lawyer's appointment book would at least show the time of day that the will signing appointment was made. There was no evidence of the time that the homemade will was signed.

After some expensive preliminary proceedings and the intervention of a mediator, Constance and the boys arrived at a settlement, from which Constance got the better end.

The lesson that Keith carried away from this is the one that led to his sharing his story. In his own words: "If only Dad had waited until after midnight to sign the will he made at home, it would have been dated the next day. If only that had happened, we wouldn't have been caught in the legal swamp that we found ourselves in."

16. PLEASE REVIEW MY SIMPLE WILL

A gentleman came into our office with a copy of his will. He had made it on his own, without legal assistance. He was certain that it was more than adequate to cover his needs, since he was in his sixties, unmarried, and had no children. His parents had passed away. He was an only child. However, as a matter of precaution, he had brought his will in so that I could review what it said just to be sure it was going to hold water. Unfortunately, he trivialized what wills lawyers do for their clients. When I asked him why he did a will on his own, he said it was because his situation was so simple.

I will now share with you, in general terms, what his homemade will said.

His handwritten will contained only two sentences. The first appointed his mother's friend as his executor. The second said that his estate was being divided "between my best friends and the relatives I feel closest to." The will was signed by him, but there was no date on it.

Aside from the fact that the will had no date and was missing important legal clauses found in lawyer-prepared wills, the two sentences contained in his will had potential problems written all over them.

His mother's friend was named as his executor, but when I asked him how old she was, he said that she was 86. There was no alternate executor named to act if she was unable to. When I pointed out to him that this was a potential problem, he responded that she was a strong woman and would probably live to be 100. He was not interested in naming a back-up executor.

He also seemed surprised when I told him that, from a will-drafting point of view, the wording in the second sentence of his will was not good. I told him that this wording was too vague. I explained that any of his friends could say that he or she was one of his "best friends." I also asked him to tell me how anyone would ever be able to prove which relatives were the "ones he felt closest to."

The gentleman retorted that I was making a mountain out of a mole hill because his executor would easily know what he meant. I asked him how the executor would know. The gentleman responded, "What are you talking about? Of course my executor would know who gets a piece of my estate!"

I asked him whether he spoke to the executor on a regular basis. He said that he didn't speak to the executor very often but he said that he knows the executor would "ask around" and get the answer. I told him that he was creating a recipe for a real battle between his friends and his relatives. But he said that he did not want to keep changing his will every time he had a falling out with a friend or a relative. He also added that with the way his will was worded, no one would ever have hurt feelings about being left out of the clause which divided up his estate, since no one was named in it.

There was no convincing this gentleman that he was on the wrong track. He simply seemed to be unable to envision various beneficiaries fighting one another as to who qualified to inherit and who did not. His final comment was, "Let them all move into my house after I'm gone. Who cares? I'll be dead anyway!"

17. RULING FROM THE GRAVE

We get to hear of very unusual situations that arise when people pass away. One of the strangest situations came to our attention when we received a call from a lawyer in another jurisdiction. He had read one of our previous books and knew we would be interested in hearing what he was experiencing as he was attempting to probate his client's estate.

What made his work so difficult were the unusual provisions contained in the will which he was being asked to probate.

For the purposes of expressing the incredible language of that will in as simple a way as possible, let us refer to the person who passed away as "Joe" and we will refer to his will as "Joe's will."

Joe appointed his brother Fred as executor. The problem with the wording of the will was that Fred's appointment would only be effective when Fred did two things. First, Fred would have to stop drinking. Second, Fred would have to show proof that he had joined Alcoholics Anonymous. Fred's appointment as executor would be of no effect if he failed to fulfill either of these two conditions.

There was no back-up executor named in the event that Fred failed to qualify.

The lawyer said that he was investigating whether the clause was legally valid. If it was, he had to find out whether Fred could ever qualify to fill that role.

Joe's will said that he had to be cremated and his ashes had to be deposited in the pond on the eighth fairway of his golf course.

Joe's will left $10,000 to his "know-it-all" sister, thanking her for all of her unending and unsolicited advice over the years. However, according to his will, his sister could not get her money from Joe's estate unless she first placed a half-page ad in the local paper thanking Joe for the money.

Joe's will left his home to his daughter, provided that she married a professional man, and only if that marriage took place after she turned 30 years of age.

His will left his coin collection to the first grandson born to any of his children, provided that this first grandson is named Joe.

His will left the rest of his estate to his son, but the executor would have to hold this gift in trust for his son until he graduated from medical school. If his son didn't graduate from medical school, then his son would not get his inheritance or any part of it until he turned sixty.

The lawyer who called us said that he had never seen such effort to rule from the grave. He said that Joe evidently wanted to stay on in this world, and departing it didn't seem to fit into Joe's personal agenda.

18. OOPS

Sometimes, one of the best gifts a person can receive is the one he or she never expected. The following story comes from one of the couples who attended a seminar we gave in a local bookstore.

Lillia and Donald started their family when they were both in their twenties. However, when Donald was turning 49 and Lillia was just past her 44th birthday, Lillia became pregnant with their third child.

Her pregnancy was an unintended one. Lillia and Donald found themselves shopping for their new baby many years after they had enjoyed a comfortable routine in their family life. While their friends told them about their Caribbean vacations and other exciting events in their lives, Lillia and Donald's world centered on night-time feedings and diaper changes for their baby boy. Despite what appeared to be a sacrifice, they treasured their new arrival.

During one of their private conversations, Lillia and Donald came up with their own nickname for their baby. His name was Donald Jr., but secretly, between themselves, they gave him the nickname "Oops." They never intended that anyone else would know of this nickname. Eventually, however, despite their best efforts at secrecy, the nickname leaked out and everyone in the family began to call Donald Jr. "Oops."

At first, Lillia and Donald felt that this name might embarrass their son. But as he grew up, he came to love his nickname.

As it turned out, over the years, Oops was one of the greatest gifts mom and dad were ever given. He was more of a devoted son to them than any of his siblings. He grew up to have an excellent academic and professional reputation. He became a respected engineer. He had, on so many occasions, shown his love, kindness, caring, and loyalty to his parents.

There was a special bond between Oops and his parents. While Donald and Lillia loved all of their children, Oops was the child who had earned their deepest friendship and trust. It was for this reason that Donald Sr. and Lillia decided to name Oops as the sole executor of both of their wills.

We like to think that we can plan the events that affect our lives, but sometimes special events occur that we never predict. To Lillia and Donald, there was a purpose for their special gift that was more important than the date that their son entered their lives.

19. MY NEPHEW IS A THIEF

James bought a vintage Mercedes car in the late 1970's. His brother, Henry, who he was very close to, was with James when he bought the car. At the time, James was a widower. However, he remarried a few years later. Unfortunately, before long, this second marriage began to fall apart. To protect the Mercedes in the looming divorce proceedings, he asked his brother Henry to make the following arrangements between themselves as brothers.

The true owner of the Mercedes would always be James, but James would sign papers so it would look like Henry owned the car, instead of himself. That way, if James's second wife tried to take the car as part of the divorce proceedings, she would fail because Henry could show that he was the owner of the car. Henry agreed to this, and the papers were signed, with the verbal understanding between the two brothers that after all the dust settled from the divorce, James would get the car back from his brother.

After a couple of years, James and his second wife finally resolved all of the divorce issues and releases were signed. However, James's problems did not end there because now he had concerns about business creditors, and, therefore, left the car in Henry's name. James had full trust in his brother.

It took James another year-and-a-half to resolve his creditor problems. It was shortly after that, however, when Henry unexpectedly passed away.

Henry's will left everything he owned to his only son, Rodney. At this point, James asked his nephew, Rodney, to sign the papers necessary to give title to the car back to him. But Rodney refused, and claimed ownership of the car because it was registered in his father's name, and that he was inheriting everything under his father's will. Rodney did not want to hear his Uncle James's explanation about James being the true owner of the car. Rodney simply wanted to keep the car for himself. James knew that Henry had told Rodney of these arrangements, but as far as Rodney was concerned, his deceased father was the owner of the car, and he was going to take it for his own.

James could not believe that his own nephew was going to steal his car. When James confronted his nephew, saying that the car was always held by Henry for him, the nephew said, "Prove it." Facing what was going to be an expensive and uphill battle, James gave up on the car. He said that the lesson to be learned was to always, always make sure there is paperwork to support what you are doing, even when you think a handshake is good enough. You may be able to trust your own brother, but that doesn't mean you can trust his heirs.

20. BUT MOM WANTED ME TO HAVE THE JEWELLERY

Doreen's fondest memories were of those rainy afternoons, sitting with her mother in her mother's bedroom. Mom would take down the wooden jewellery cases from the top shelf of her bedroom closet, and they would spread out Grandma's bracelets, rings, necklaces, and pins on the bedspread. Doreen and her Mom would hold the pieces up to the light and Mom would tell Doreen about "how Grandma loved to wear this necklace or that ring." Mom would talk about the family gatherings where she herself wore the pieces that Grandma had handed down to her. Mom would often tell Doreen that the treasured family jewellery, with all of its history, would be in Doreen's hands one day. Mom promised Doreen that she would eventually inherit all of this jewellery. She assured Doreen that her will provided for this. She even showed Doreen her will.

Mom's will left her entire estate to Dad, but if Dad died first, Mom's will provided that all of her jewellery would go to Doreen, and the rest of Mom's estate would be divided equally between Doreen and her two brothers.

As logical as this sounds, the provision made in Mom's will about the jewellery going to Doreen amounted to no more than empty promises because of the events that happened to Doreen's family, which neither Doreen nor her mother expected. These events ended up creating a bitter war between Doreen and her brothers.

Mom and Dad were in a serious car accident. Mom died in that accident and Dad survived her, leaving him in a coma because of his serious injuries. Not long afterward, these injuries resulted in his death.

Doreen was still mourning her parents' deaths when her brothers pressed her to go to the lawyer's office to discuss the estate. The lawyer explained to her that her Dad's will appointed her two brothers as his executors, and that this will divided his estate equally among his three children. She asked the lawyer about Mom's jewellery. The lawyer showed Doreen that her father's will made no mention of jewellery.

It did not take Doreen long to realize that had Mom outlived Dad, she would have inherited the jewellery according to what Mom's will said. But when it came to her inheriting the jewellery, her parents died in the wrong order. As a result, all of Mom's jewellery, which included Grandma's jewellery, was inherited by Dad. When Doreen's Dad passed away, his will simply split his estate equally among his three children, which meant that the jewellery was now one-third Doreen's and two-thirds belonged to her brothers.

The battle between Doreen and her brothers began when the jewellery was appraised as part of the administration of Dad's estate. That was when Doreen and her brothers learned that the value of this jewellery exceeded $125,000. Her brothers were happy to have Doreen take the jewellery, but this would end up costing her $83,000 and not a dime less.

At first, Doreen tried to reason with her brothers. She told them that Mom wanted her to have the jewellery and that they always knew it, because Mom told them so. She told them that Mom had specified this in her will in the clearest possible language. She told them that Mom would have been shocked and disappointed if she knew that her two sons were trying to force Doreen to buy the jewellery from them.

But Doreen's brothers said that their lawyer told them to only look at their father's will, and that Mom's will did not count anymore, because Dad had outlived Mom.

She responded that if Dad had not been so seriously injured in the accident, he would definitely have changed his will to follow what Mom's will said.

Doreen's brothers argued back that it was too bad, but the law is the law. Dad outlived Mom, his will clearly split everything between all three children, and that included the jewellery because Mom's will left it to Dad. They took an uncompromising stance and would not give in an inch to her.

Doreen wanted the jewellery and told her brothers that she would reluctantly give in to their extortion, and accept a reduction of her share of the remainder of Mom's estate to satisfy their greed. She told them that she would never forget that they were taking advantage of the order of the deaths of Mom and Dad. She said that they were profiting from a twist of fate and that she was disgusted at how they were disrespecting Mom.

In the end, Doreen's share in Mom's estate was reduced by the $83,000. In order to get this share, she had to sign a release document. She signed it, as her brothers asked, but at the bottom of the release, she wrote, "I'll never forget what you did to me and I will always remember your words, 'the law is the law,' but the law can't force me to ever speak to either of you again!"

21. I CAN'T BELIEVE MY KIDS DID THIS TO ME: A WARNING FROM A HURT MOTHER

A distraught woman called us when we were guests on a radio show, with a warning to other parents not to fall into the trap that she found herself in.

When times were good, she and her husband had loaned large sums to each of their children. Their daughter received $100,000 and their son received $150,000. She said that this money helped to save her daughter's marriage and her son's business. She said that both children vowed to pay back the money. Both children were warm and grateful at the time.

Several years after those loans to her children, her personal situation changed drastically. Her husband sold his business to someone who gave him a partial down payment. Before long, that purchaser went bankrupt and could not pay anything more to her husband. The family business was gone, with very little to show for a lifetime of work. Then her husband passed away. He left his estate to her, but there was very little to it.

The caller explained that because of these events, she found herself in a serious financial bind. She told us that, in order to maintain herself, she desperately needed the money she had loaned to her children. She said that it was unfair that a person of her age had to work six days a week as a cashier in a grocery store, and then to also moonlight for an evening shift in a fast food restaurant.

When she pleaded with her daughter to see if at least some of the money that was loaned to her could be repaid, her daughter became very angry. She said that for her, repayment was impossible because of her own financial problems. She explained to her mother that if she tried to set aside any money to pay her back, it would be the straw that broke the camel's back for her marriage.

When the caller asked her son for some repayment, his response was even worse. He lost his temper, and told her that the $150,000 he received was a gift, not a loan. Now our caller didn't know what to do. When she insisted that the money he received was a loan, her son said, "Prove it." She said she and her husband had trusted their children and had never bothered to get anything in writing for the money their children borrowed from them. Her words to us were, "Now look where I am because of that."

The caller said that if she wanted the money back from her children, her only option was to sue them, but that the stress and embarrassment of doing something like this would be unbearable. She began to cry and finished her call by saying that the least she could do was to warn all of the parents out there who might be listening, to always document any loans they make to their children. She verbalized her warning to the listening audience as follows: "They may be your children and you may think you will always be able to trust them. However, please know that situations and people can change. If you ever need the money back from them, a loan document is at least some form of protection."

22. ISN'T IT A BEAUTIFUL DAY?

Rachel's chronic heart condition had kept her in her hospital room for weeks on end. Her other ailments had kept her housebound for months before this. Her doctor had made no secret that she only had a few months left to live. It was under these conditions that Rachel called our office from her hospital bed. She wanted to make her will. She had the blessing of her doctor to spend a few hours outside the hospital. She made it clear to me that she was going to be driven to our office in a van, and that she could not get out of that van, because of her weak physical condition. I agreed that I would meet Rachel in that van, in order to take her instructions to prepare her will.

I remember that autumn day when I stepped into that van to meet with her. It was drizzling slightly and the sky was dark. Aside from being a dreary, damp day, it was also the type of day when traffic was heavy, even at the noon hour. There had been a traffic accident which delayed my drive back to the office. I had felt tension, partly from the delay and partly from the horns that were blaring from frustrated drivers.

Even back at the office, every client seemed to feel that his or her problem was urgent, and had to be a first priority. The faxes, e-mails, and voicemails all seemed to come at once. If there was ever a day where a person might have a short temper, this was it.

Rachel's appointment was in the middle of the afternoon. My secretary called me on the intercom to tell me that my client in the van had just arrived in our parking lot.

I went out to the parking lot, holding an umbrella. Through the passenger window I could see a woman smiling. The driver came out to greet me. She whispered that she was Rachel's friend, and that the woman in the passenger seat was Rachel. She also said that this was the first time Rachel had been outside in months. She went on to tell me that with the condition Rachel was in, she didn't know if Rachel would ever be outside again.

As I got into the driver's seat of that van, I introduced myself to Rachel. She looked at me, smiled, and said that it was nice to meet me. I remember being a little surprised to see that her window was rolled down, because it was raining. I was even more surprised when she looked away, stretching her arm outside the window, into the cold drizzle. The rain was falling on her bare hand. After about a minute, she turned back to me and said, in a voice that was almost singing, "Isn't it a beautiful day?" Her words touched something deep inside me. I suddenly realized that this day meant two entirely different things to each of us. The dreary weather had been a heavy weight on my mood. The weather had also negatively affected the moods of those I had encountered throughout the day. However, since Rachel's world consisted of being confined to a hospital room for what little life she had left, this cold and wet outing seemed to provide her with a wellspring of joy.

Rachel signed her will that day, out there in the van. Less than two weeks later, the friend who had driven her to my office parking lot called to tell me that Rachel had passed away.

"Isn't it a beautiful day?"...

Sometimes, a few words can speak volumes.

23. HE BLEW IT FOR THE FAMILY

Charles built up the motel business over 40 years of toiling 7 days a week. The business became a success and he supported his family over many years. He eventually brought his son Andrew into the business. They did not see eye-to-eye on everything; but they were father and son, and under Charles' guidance, the motel continued to prosper.

The day came when Charles felt confident enough to turn over the management of his motel business to Andrew. At this point in time, the business was profitable enough to support Charles, his wife, his daughter and her family, and, of course, Andrew and his family.

For the next eighteen months, everything went according to plan. But under Andrew's management, the business began to deteriorate. As the profits fell, tensions grew between father and son. Charles told Andrew that he was running the business recklessly, and could not read the writing on the wall.

At first, father and son kept this between themselves, but the business was headed for failure, and, eventually, the motel went into bankruptcy. Everything was auctioned off piece-by-piece. The failure of their business had a devastating effect on the lifestyles of the entire family. Charles and his wife had to sell their home of 30 years, and move into a small condominium. Andrew lost his home. His sister and her husband, who were both working in the motel and also relied upon the business financially, had to sell their home, and move into a rental property.

The tension between Charles and his son Andrew created a wall of silence between them. They spoke to each other only when they had no alternative. About a year after the failure of the motel business, the whole family attended a cousin's wedding, and it was at this wedding that the silence between Charles and Andrew was broken.

It was common knowledge among the relatives that under Andrew's management, the motel business had failed. When the groom came by the table with his new bride, he gracefully mentioned that he missed dropping in on the motel. "I guess you guys got caught up in the drop in tourism," he said. But that comment was the tipping point for Charles, who had been choking back his fury for over a year.

Now it all came out. Charles told the groom and the family sitting around the table that the failure of the motel had nothing to do with a drop in tourism. "I ran that business for forty years through good times and bad," he said. "That idiot son of mine gets his hands on the business for a year-and-a-half and kills what I built up over 40 years. I told him that I didn't want to borrow money, but he said that he had a business administration degree from a university and that I should trust him. He persuaded me to borrow a million dollars from the bank, and, for what? To put in another fifty rooms that we could not fill? To put large screen TV's in every room? Did he have to spend tens of thousands of dollars renovating the old rooms and to pay a fortune for a useless exterior facelift? My stupid son, here, is the one who threw away his inheritance and his sister's as well!" With that, Andrew yelled back, "Dad was born a genius. Of course, Dad never made a mistake in his life. If anything ever went wrong, it was always my fault."

The father retorted, "The only mistake I made was trusting you." Those words were the last ever spoken between father and son, as the son stormed out of the room and out of the lives of the rest of the family.

24. FROM PEACE SIGNS TO DOLLAR SIGNS

A woman phoned in on one of our call-in shows to vent her anger over what her younger brother had done to her.

She began by describing her brother, who she said was a peace-loving idealist in the late 1960's. He joined a volunteer organization that provided aid to the sick and impoverished in Africa. When he came back from Africa, the focus of his life was to do everything possible to help the poor. He also marched with his fellow hippies in the anti-war movement.

When their father confronted her brother about his utopian view of life, and told him to get a real job, her brother called their father a capitalist pig. He often ridiculed their father, accusing him of only caring about money, not people. She remembered how much this hurt their father.

In the 1970's, their mother passed away. In the 1980's, their father died.

When it came to dividing their father's estate, our caller found that her brother was a changed person. She was the executor of her father's estate, and she was responsible for looking after the affairs of the estate, distributing what their father owned. While she was doing her best to administer the estate, her brother was constantly pestering her for an accounting. She had to hire a bookkeeper to help her prepare the estate accounts, and when she gave her brother the full details in a neat package, he complained that she was hiding estate assets from him and that she was covering up something, implying that she was stealing from her father's estate.

Her brother demanded to see every single original invoice and bill paid from the estate. He told her she should not charge anything for her work, and ignored the hours and hours she had spent. He said he would fight her if she tried to claim any compensation for her work as executor. She said that not only was she not taking anything from the estate, but on the other hand, she had spent many months of her life as a caregiver for their father, without asking her brother for anything, and without complaining. She never told her brother that he was not doing his fair share to help Dad.

She went on to talk about the way in which her brother decided to become active in the affairs of her father's estate. When it came to the silver and the crystal in the home, he seemed to be reaching for everything he could get his hands on, and he reached much further than she ever expected.

She came to learn from her sister-in-law, that her brother had grand plans for his inheritance. He was not giving it to charity. He was going to sell his home and buy a much larger one, and that he was also going to buy sports cars for himself and his wife.

The caller said that now she knew her brother for what he had turned out to be: a money-grabbing hypocrite, no longer the peace-loving hippie everyone thought he was. She ended the call by saying, "My brother used to call my father a capitalist pig. He was wrong. The pig is my brother. Evidently, he has completely forgotten who he was and what he had stood for in his twenties."

25. WHO THEY SAVED IT FOR

Sometimes we read about a sad situation where a business fails. This story is about sadness that entered into the lives of a husband and wife who had a successful business.

Every single weekday morning, for over twenty-five years, Carole woke her husband, Moe, at 4:30. Moe would open their corner store at 6:00 in the morning, and the store would close about 11:00 every night. They shared their workdays. Carole would look after their only child, Victor, every day until 4:30 in the afternoon. Then she would leave for the store to arrive there about 5:00 in the afternoon. Then Moe would come home for supper to look after Victor. Carole would work until closing time and lock the store up for the night.

A close friend who lived across the street would help them with Victor during the time that both Carole and Moe had to be out of the house.

Carole and Moe did with their own two hands, whatever it took to run the business. Whether it was balancing the books, or purchasing fruits and vegetables, cleaning the floors, or stocking the shelves, they did it all. One of them worked Saturdays and the other worked Sundays. They would alternate this way on the weekends. There was no time to take vacations.

As the years passed, Victor grew up to be their pride and joy. He was the main reason for their years of working long hours and saving. They spent very little money on themselves, but they always found the money to pay for Victor's needs, whether it was for his music lessons, his sports equipment, his clothing, or for anything else he required.

Carole and Moe would often fantasize about how one day, Victor would marry and have children. They imagined grandchildren playing in their home. This is what they lived for.

Victor was doing well at his university, and his goal was to become a doctor. Carole and Moe vowed that whatever it took, even if it took their last dollar, Victor's tuition would be paid. They wanted Victor to have an easier life than they had.

One night, about a week after they helped Victor celebrate his graduation from the university, their sleep was interrupted by a knock on the front door. They opened the door to a policeman in uniform. He had some very sad news for them. He asked them if they could all sit down. The policeman seemed to struggle to find words. Finally, he told them that there had been an accident and a young man was tragically killed in the accident. The police found Victor's identification in the young man's wallet. The policeman needed Carole and Moe to identify the body.

"Distraught" is too pale a word to describe how Carole and Moe felt. The driving force behind all their hard work, their hopes, and their dreams was suddenly taken from them.

Their sad story poured out to me through their tears, as we met for them to make new wills. In their previous wills, Carole and Moe left everything to each other, and when they both died, Victor was going to inherit their estates.

They said that when they made those wills several years ago, what was very important to them was that they were leaving more than money to Victor. They were leaving a piece of themselves to someone who would understand what their many years of sacrifice meant. Carole described the image she had in her mind, of Victor telling the children he was supposed to have, of how hard their grandparents had worked during their lives, so that they might have a good life. Now, a cruel tragedy had taken this image from her.

Before their tragic loss, Carole and Moe had never imagined that they would have to leave their estates to anyone other than Victor. Carole described how she felt. "We go through the motions every day like before but there isn't any life in what we do or what we feel. We are dead leaves blowing around in the wind."

According to their new wills, after Carole and Moe both died, their estates would be left to Moe's cousin Flora. Flora had recently come out of a personal bankruptcy. She was in her mid-fifties and Carole and Moe felt that the inheritance would be of great help to someone they cared about.

As she was signing her will, Carole said, "We like Flora, but she will never really appreciate what Moe and I went through for decades, to get the money that she'll be inheriting. All of what we worked for was supposed to go to Victor and the family he should have had."

The story continues. About a year later, Carole and Moe came back to my office to once again, make new wills. This time, they told me that now they wanted to delete Flora from their wills, and everything they had was going to be left to their Church, to help the poorest of the congregation. Carole explained that during the time of their deepest despair and depression, they were able to turn to their Church for support.

I told Carole that I respected her for her decision but I was duty bound to ask why she changed her mind about Flora. She explained.

"After Moe and I did our wills, we agreed not to tell anyone about what we wrote in them, so Flora had no way of knowing what our wills said. It was by a coincidence that Flora called us and wanted to introduce her new boyfriend to us.

When we met, she told us that the two of them were trying to start a new business and needed about $30,000 to get it going. Flora asked us if we could loan the money to them. Moe and I were taken by surprise and embarrassed, especially because Flora put us on the spot in front of her boyfriend who she had just introduced to us. We said that we'd have to think about it. Flora got mad, and said, 'Victor's gone! Who are you saving it for?'

Moe and I didn't argue with her. We said we would get back to her. Flora should have known the pain she caused us with that comment."

Carole was visibly upset as she told me this. It seemed that anything that brought back the memories of her son made her cry.

After they signed their new wills, Moe said that they felt that they were doing the right thing. He said, "Since Victor passed away, we have been living with an emptiness that we tried to fill in any way we could. Our closure is that our years of hard work will end up helping those that are in need. We know that this is what Victor would have wanted."

26. UNCLE'S UNIQUE WILL-PLANNING TECHNIQUE

A caller to a radio show told us a very unusual story.

She spoke of her elderly uncle who was a widower with no children, but who had many nieces and nephews. He was an eccentric, wealthy man. What was so unique about her story was that her uncle, who could hear very well, went to great lengths to give the general impression that he was very hard of hearing. As the story went, he was successful in his efforts. His pretended hearing impairment lulled those in his presence into a false sense of security; but the reality was that he was able to hear things which others did not think he would be able to hear.

Our caller said that her uncle confided in her that he initially developed this unusual tactic for his business purposes, but by the time he was in his mid-eighties, he began to use it in family gatherings, in the company of his nieces and nephews. As a result, their unguarded dialogue spoke volumes to her uncle.

Over a period of time, the comments made during Christmas and Thanksgiving dinners and other informal gatherings of the family, gave her uncle a clear vision as to those who had genuine affection for him on the one hand, and those whose greed, disrespect, and lack of concern for him showed them to be undeserving of his generosity.

Of all of his nieces and nephews, our caller was the only one who had earned the trust of her uncle. This is why her uncle decided to confide in her about his hearing ability. She laughed as she described the night when many truths came out. It was at her uncle's 90th birthday party, when all of his nieces and nephews were gathered together. When her uncle stood up to give a few words of thanks to the family, he surprised them when the first thing he said was, "I've been waiting to say these words for the last few years: I can hear perfectly. I have always had perfect hearing, and I have heard everything you have ever said to me and about me." That shocked everyone in the room. Then he turned to his nieces and nephews, one-by-one and said:

to Gregory, "So I understand that you really can't wait to get your hands on my large screen TV;"

and to Nancy, "I'm sorry you think I'm so cheap;"

and to Paul, "So you think it's a pain in the neck to have to drive me to the doctor's office;"

and to Claire, "I'm sorry I'm such a burden to you, or as you said, 'a real pain in the ***.' "

The comments from the uncle to the nieces and nephews went on and on until they each had heard what they thought their uncle had not.

Our caller could hardly restrain herself from laughing on the radio in describing the astonished looks on the faces of eight of her cousins, who had spent all this time thinking their uncle was practically deaf. In the end, our caller's uncle confided in her that he now knew exactly what would be in his will.

27. IT'S ABOUT TIME (GRANDPA'S WATCH)

In or about the year 1954, Brian's family wanted to do something special for the 85th birthday party they were planning for Grandpa. Between brothers, sisters, cousins, children, and grandchildren, well over 75 people were involved in this celebration. While it was not going to be a surprise party, the relatives still wanted a surprise element to bring a smile to everybody who would be celebrating this momentous event with Grandpa.

Grandma's sister was a business woman who travelled a lot. She was the one who was chosen by the family to buy an expensive gold watch as a special birthday gift for Grandpa. All of the closer relatives were happy to contribute their share to her so that Grandma's sister would have all the money she needed to buy only the very best for Grandpa.

At the birthday party, Grandpa was totally taken by surprise when the gold watch was presented to him. You could see the smile in his eyes. There were hugs, kisses, and applause. There was even a special mention of thanks for Grandma's sister, for all the trouble and effort she went through to get this very special watch for Grandpa and for keeping the secret. Brian remembered all of this. He was in his mid-teens at the time.

After Grandpa died, Brian's dad inherited the watch. His dad kept the watch in its original wooden case. Brian's dad told him that if anything ever happened to him, Brian should know that the watch was in that wooden box, on the upper shelf of Dad's closet. Dad rarely took the watch out, and wore it only on the most formal of occasions. Dad was not only proud of that watch, but also took pride in the fact that of all of the relatives, he was the one who was chosen by Grandpa to get that special watch when Grandpa died.

Brian knew that for the rest of his dad's life, the watch was his father's prized possession. More than once, his dad had told Brian that he heard that Grandma's sister had collected over $3,000 from the family when she went on the road to find that watch back in the 1950's. Back then, $3,000 was an enormous amount of money for a watch.

When his dad passed away, Brian was deeply moved that his dad had left the watch to him, and not to his two brothers. He knew that this angered his brothers, but Brian did not want to have a fight over this.

He told his brothers that he wanted to resolve this watch issue with them. Brian remembered how suspicious his brothers seemed when he mentioned this to them. Brian insisted though, and brought the watch to an appraiser. He told the appraisal to handle this special watch with care because it apparently cost over $3,000 in the 1950's and a gold watch like this must be worth a lot more today.

After a few days, the appraiser called to tell him that the appraisal was ready and that he could pick up the watch. As he was picking up the watch from the appraiser, Brian said that he felt a sense of relief that nothing had happened to the watch between leaving the safety of his home and getting it back into his hands.

The appraiser looked at Brian with a smile on his face. "Look at the appraisal," he said. Brian put the watch on his wrist and opened up the envelope. The appraisal was for $389 for a watch with a gold-filled band.

What shocked Brian more than this appraisal was the fact that Grandma's sister got away with pocketing the family's money and fooling both his grandfather and his father.

When Brian showed the appraisal to his two brothers, their laughter healed any wounds that their dad's will might have originally created.

They laughed even harder when they all decided that they would make a special gift of this watch for Grandma's sister's granddaughter who had just invited them to her wedding.

28. "AND THE CALLER SAID…" (SOME SURPRISING TELEPHONE CALLS WE'VE RECEIVED)

CALLER A. She called to say that her father had recently passed away. After the reading of his will, she discovered that the family home was left to her. Her question to us was, "When can I tell my brother and my sister that they can never set foot in the home again?"

CALLER B. The caller was a beneficiary under a will. He embarked on a long story about how he felt that the executor was dragging his feet and was not administering the estate quickly enough. He himself had bills to pay, needed the inheritance money, and wanted advice as to how he could get the executor to do his job.

When I asked him when the deceased passed away, the caller said, "He was buried four days ago."

CALLER C. The caller said that his brother died last month and he was named as executor to look after the estate. He said that his sister called a few days after the funeral, which she did not attend. Her only question to him was, "I understand that you are the executor. When do I get my inheritance?" This was the first time anyone in the family had heard from her in the last 20 years.

CALLER D. The caller told us about his 82-year-old mother and asked, "How can I get out of the personal guarantee I signed with Mom's nursing home? When I signed it, I figured she'd never make it past 80. I never thought she would live this long."

CALLER E. The caller took me by surprise when he asked, "Will it help my case against my brother if I can prove he cheated on his wife?"

CALLER F. She called to say that she wanted to sue her executor brother, and went on to say, "I hate Bill. He's not my real brother. He's adopted."

CALLER G. The caller said, "I think I have 5 kids. Do I have to include all of them in my will?" This surprised me, and I asked, "Why do you THINK you have 5?"

"Because I have not seen any of them since my divorce 30 years ago, and I don't know if they are alive or dead."

CALLER H. We were acting for a client who was fighting his sister. She was not represented by any lawyer. On one occasion his sister called our office and left the following message on our voicemail: "I'll never give in to his demands. Next time you speak to my brother, please tell him how much I hate him."

CALLER I. In discussing his lawsuit, the caller asked, "If I delay long enough and my brother dies, is the case over?"

CALLER J. The caller was the executor of his mother's estate. His brother was demanding an immediate accounting of what was going on in her estate. When I told him that he did have a duty to account to all of the beneficiaries, the caller came up with this surprising explanation for ignoring his brother's demands: "That miserable S.O.B. stole from me and now I am going to steal it back from him, and if he doesn't like it then he can sue me."

CALLER K: We heard from a caller on a radio show, speaking about her cousin, whom she described as cold, selfish, and disgusting. The caller was describing the daughter of her recently deceased aunt. According to the caller, her aunt lived at home and coped all alone with her terminal illness, up to the day she passed away.

The caller talked about a visit she made to her aunt's home shortly before her aunt passed away. Her cousin also happened to be visiting the home at the same time. During this visit, she asked her cousin, "Have you thought about hiring a caregiver to help your Mom do the cooking and the cleaning to give your Mom some relief?" Her cousin answered, "No way! Do you have any idea how much that can cost?"

The caller went on to tell us that her cousin was "a disgusting human being." We asked why. She said, "I told you that she wouldn't hire a caregiver for her mother because it was too expensive. Yet less than three weeks after her mother's death, I saw her driving a new Cadillac. I wonder where she got the money."

CALLER L. The caller said that her brother bragged to the entire family of how he never skipped a single day, visiting Mom in the hospital while Mom was sick. "Sure, my brother was there," the caller said, pointing out that she was with her mother at the hospital every day, "but hospital visiting hours ended at 8:00 p.m. and he made sure that he never arrived there before 7:45 p.m.!"

CALLER M. "My brother is a blood-sucking parasite!" the caller exclaimed, as she described how great an actor and fraudster her brother was. She spoke of how her brother would cough and cough over and over in the presence of their mother. He also made sure their mother saw him limp and struggle to walk. She spoke of how sorry Mom felt for her brother and how he was fooling her. She went on to speak of the new car Mom bought for him to help him get around, and about the expensive Arizona vacation she paid for so he could recover from his coughing. The caller sounded frustrated and defeated when she asked, "How can I prove that my brother isn't really sick? At this rate, there will be nothing left for me."

CALLER N. A lawyer called us when we were on a radio show. He said that his client was engaged in a vicious fight with a brother, over a minor amount of money. He told his client that his legal fees will probably be more than the amount that the client was fighting over. His client said money was no object, and that his fight was a matter of principle. The lawyer told us that his client would willingly pay "thousands" in his attempt to recover what he felt his brother owed him. Then the lawyer turned his call into a question, as he asked us: "How much money do you think this fight involves?"

We tried to guess what the amount might be: "$3,000? $4,000?" "No," said the lawyer, "less than $300."

29. I'M KICKING MYSELF

We heard the following story at a seminar from a middle-aged man who came up to us during a break. His mother's will left everything to him and his two siblings equally. He went on to say that her will also contained a clause which forgave all of the debts any of her children owed to her. He asked if this forgiveness clause was usually found in a will. We answered that it was always up to the person making the will to decide whether or not to forgive debts. We also mentioned that from our experience, this clause is used only in a small minority of the wills that we have prepared or probated.

He seemed downcast in hearing that this special clause in his mother's will was not one which was universally used by people making wills. He then continued with his story.

Several years before his mother had passed away, he had borrowed $10,000 from her. Now we were puzzled by the fact that he appeared to be downcast over this because his mother's will said that the money he borrowed did not have to be paid back. This made no sense to us until he told the rest of his story.

He said that a few years before his mother passed away, his brother had borrowed $200,000 from their mother, to buy a home. The man telling the story was not angry at his brother for this, but has been kicking himself ever since his mother died, telling us that once he realized that her will had this debt forgiveness clause, he should have borrowed much more money from Mom when he had the chance.

30. THE PENNY MINE SHARES

Often, we speak of "the estate" of a person who had passed away and left everything he or she owned to one or more people or charitable organizations. Many of the stories you have read up to this point have dealt with how an estate was distributed, or about who was entitled to what.

Unless a person accumulates money, property, or other assets, there will be little or nothing to distribute once the person has passed away. A person who makes poor decisions in managing his or her affairs may leave an estate which falls into this category. Sometimes, however, the question of whether a person dies rich or poor may be more a matter of luck than of skill. My father told me the following story about a friend of his. This story demonstrates the power of blind luck.

Wayne returned to his university studies in the fall after his summer job working in the mining country. During his summer job, he had come to know many of the miners. One of the rumours that had circulated among them was about a massive mineral deposit that one of the smaller mining companies had discovered.

Wayne saw that this small company was listed on the local stock exchange at six cents a share. He decided to take a chance on the rumour he heard and so he bought 100,000 shares.

Not long after his purchase, he beamed when the stock was at eight cents - a gain of two cents a share. He was so proud of his good judgement that he began to tell his friends that he had bought thousands of shares of this little company and had already made some real money.

His words were taken very seriously by these friends, who bought the same quantity of shares that Wayne had bought.

The stock continued its climb from eight cents, then to twelve cents, but then it began to fluctuate. Twelve became nine, then five, then three. At this low stock price point, Wayne became nervous about the advice that he had given to his friends. Despite his fear, he told them that he was "along for the ride." Once again, they followed his instincts.

There was no relief from the roller coaster movement of this stock for weeks upon end. Then suddenly, the stock went to fourteen cents, then to twenty cents, then to forty, then to a dollar. His friends were ecstatic as the stock achieved new heights.

Week after week the stock would increase in value, and every Friday during this time, first one friend, and then another would arrange a party to celebrate their newfound wealth. Months later, the stock hit five dollars and forty cents. At that time, Wayne's friends told him that they were going to cash in all of their shares and take their huge profits. They wanted to celebrate their newfound wealth with an expensive party on a chartered yacht and they should all pitch in to share their bonanza. They suggested an even split among them.

Now, for the first time since the beginning of this adventure, Wayne had to say, "No." His friends were insistent. They had all made a fortune, hadn't they? Not Wayne. Wayne had to come clean. "Fellows, I have no money. I got nervous, and sold out way back when the stock was at fourteen cents."

31. A COUPLE OF INHERITANCE JOKES WE'VE HEARD

JOKE A. Harold and Tim, two baby-boomers in their mid-fifties, met for the first time in many years. They went to a quiet restaurant for lunch. After lunch, they took a long walk, and Harold began to speak from his heart about his financial struggles. "I've got a big mortgage, heavy-duty car payments, my kids' tuition, and too many credit card bills. Tim said, "I'm sorry to hear that, but for me, life has been good. I have no financial worries at all."

Harold was puzzled. "Tim," he asked, "how is it that our lives have unfolded so differently in twenty-five years? We both grew up on the same street. Your dad was a barber and mine was a shoemaker. We both wore hand-me-downs. Our fathers always drove used cars. Our families never went out to restaurants to eat. Our mothers both watched every penny. We went to high school and college together and we each needed part-time jobs to get by.

During lunch you mentioned that you have two luxury cars, an expensive home, a condominium in Florida, and a chalet in the Swiss Alps. What is it that you did that I didn't do? How did you make all that money?"

Tim took in all of this. He looked studious, serious. He took his time before answering. Finally he looked at Harold and said, "Look, I can't get into all of this, but I will tell you that I am worth about eight million dollars." Harold asked a second time, "Eight million dollars! How did you make all that money?"

Tim replied, "Okay, I will tell you how I made my first few dollars. Do you remember that apple orchard near where we lived? Well I would wake up in the morning and pick a few apples and sell them for ten cents each. Then another day, I would pick more apples and also sell them for ten cents each. Eventually, I brought a bushel with me and filled it and sold each of the apples for ten cents each."

Harold may not have been wealthy, but that did not mean that Harold couldn't count. As Harold listened to Tim, he remained puzzled.

After Tim got to the point where he had made about $150 after climbing up and down and selling bushel after bushel, Harold had to ask, "Okay Tim, I can see about $150 here. But how did you make the rest of the eight million?"

"Oh," said Tim, "that was easy. My Uncle Wilfred died and left it to me."

JOKE B. Very wealthy 75-year-old Phil marries very good looking 31-year-old Claudette.

At their wedding, Phil's best man asks him how on earth he managed to get a gorgeous woman like Claudette to marry him. Was it because of Phil's vast wealth?

"No, said Phil to his friend, that wasn't it. I lied about my age."

"What did you say?" asked his friend, anxious that Phil reveal his secret. "That you were 65, not 75?"

"No," answered Phil. "I told her that that I was 95."

32. SOME FUNNY MOMENTS

MOMENT A. The host of a radio show we were on, mentioned that our books were available from our office, by calling our toll-free number. Our secretary happened to be busy, so I took a call, which was from a woman who told me that she was in her eighties. She started by giving me a good part of her life story, including her various health problems. She said that with all of her ailments, she wanted our book on wills as soon as possible. After giving me her credit card number, she continued to tell me all about her old age and her frail health. She spoke of her heart problems, her stomach problems, and her insomnia, when I finally had to interrupt her. Her credit card information still had to be completed. I said, "I'm sorry to hear about your health problems, but there are other calls coming in that I have to answer." Returning to the issue of the credit card, I asked, "What is your expiry date?" to which the woman exclaimed, "Honey, my doctor hasn't told me yet!"

MOMENT B. A woman in her late 30's came into my office to ask about making a will. She spoke of her love for a man who was in his 80's. She described how deeply in love they were, having lived together for a few months.

"We are so much in love. I can't be without him and he can't be without me."

She described their passionate, intimate relations. She said that more than anything else in her life, what she wanted most of all was that their relationship be permanent. She kept telling me how she loved that man, that she would do anything in the world for him, and that she could not think of a life without him because he was her whole world.

It was at that point that she revealed to me that the will she wanted me to make was his will, not hers.

I replied, "Unless he instructs me to make his will himself, I can't do it." She then said, "If you can't do that, I have another suggestion. I can tell you what he wants, you can prepare the will, and I can take it back to him to get it signed." I refused, repeating that I needed him to be here to give me instructions himself.

My response seemed to upset her and she seemed disappointed to hear it. Then she said what worried her so much was that when her lover woke up that morning, he was not feeling well and was very tired. She also said that her lover was too weak to come to the office for an appointment. However, she said that she knew that he wanted her to have everything he owned.

I said that I was not able to help her. If she wanted a house call for him she would need to find another lawyer.

She said that although they were both passionately in love with one another, and had been living together for a few months, they were not yet married. Then she asked me, "By the way, what happens if he dies without a will?" I replied that under the laws of our jurisdiction, she would not be entitled to an inheritance from him. She seemed to be in shock. Evidently this was not the answer she expected to hear. Her next words were, "You mean I get nothing if he dies without a will? I get nothing!? Then why am I with him? I really don't care about him. I don't even like him. I don't even want to be with him! I'm wasting my time with him, and I'm wasting my time here with you!" And without another word, she stormed right out of the office.

MOMENT C. An elderly client told us that he had a novel way to get his grandchildren to visit his gravesite after he passed away. The gentleman said that he was thinking of arranging for an ATM machine to stand beside his headstone. He added that the only way his grandchildren would visit his gravesite was if they knew that they could get $20 from the machine, each time they visited his grave.

MOMENT D. Sometimes, an emotionally overburdened executor will ask us, on his behalf, to call a friend or a family member of the deceased, in order to break the news of the death, and to inform that person of an inheritance.

On one such call that I made, I did break the news to one of the friends of the deceased to tell him of the death of his friend, and of a $5,000 gift to him. From what my client, the executor, had told me, the person who I was asked to call was a long-time friend who the executor described to me as being "near and dear" to the deceased. When I called the long-time friend, as I was instructed to do, there was a brief silence at the other end of the line, and then the long-time friend said:

"Sorry to hear about Charlie. I'm surprised he left me anything." Then he got excited as he said, "I have so many bills to pay. The money's a godsend!"

33. GOOD NEWS

After a seminar we attended for wills and estate lawyers, there was an informal session where several of us sat around, exchanging stories about our experiences. Lawyers who talk about this sort of thing always speak in anonymous terms, of course, because even in a social gathering, we are still bound by, and very conscious of, the confidentiality of each and every client.

One of the lawyers told the following story.

He had a male client who was in his office on an urgent basis because his blood test showed that he had a serious and aggressive form of lymphoma, and he was desperate to protect his family. It was uncertain as to how long his client would live. His client was in a depressed state, and the words that the lawyer used to describe his impression of his client were: demoralized, sad, facing imminent death.

He said that his client's mood seemed to sadden the very atmosphere of his office boardroom. "It was as if the walls had turned a darker tone." He said that the hushed atmosphere in his boardroom reminded him of a funeral home. The lawyer observed that everything that had to be said was expressed in barely more than a whisper. When the secretary came in with the final draft of the client's will, the room was so quiet that he remembered how the pages sounded as they were turned.

The lawyer was almost through explaining this final draft of the will, when his client's cell phone began to vibrate. It made a buzzing sound, and all three in the deathly quiet room could clearly hear its gentle buzzing.

The client lifted the phone to his ear. In describing this moment, the lawyer said that it was impossible to hear what the caller was saying. The client looked very intent for about a minute. Then he cleared his throat and said into his cell phone, "Could you repeat that, please? COULD YOU REPEAT THAT, PLEASE??"

The client said nothing more, but his body language suddenly changed, as he snapped the telephone shut. He jumped up, his arms raised, exclaiming to the lawyer, "They made a mistake!! I'm okay!! I'm okay!!" Now he was another person altogether, and he bent over and hugged the secretary, and shook the lawyer's hand, chanting over and over, "They made a mistake. I'm okay!!"

Then, the lawyer described what happened next. The man slid the unsigned will across the boardroom table and said, "Never mind, I'm not signing anything. I'm outta here! Send me the bill."

34. DIVIDING MOTHER'S DAY

If you die without a will, and leave a spouse and children surviving you, the law in many jurisdictions will not give your spouse your entire estate. In such cases, your spouse will receive a portion of your estate, and will have to share the rest of your estate with your children.

This next story is about a father who died without a will, leaving his wife and two adult sons. This set in motion a series of events which, in the end, tore his family apart.

Jeanne came to speak to us about her husband's estate. Her husband left no will. As we began to talk about his estate, she broke down. She said that her husband's death had "unleashed a tidal wave of sorrow." Not only had she lost her husband, but his death and his failure to do a will tore apart the bond between her two sons, who had always been close right up to when their father passed away. Jeanne then explained what drove her sons apart.

After her husband's funeral, while Jeanne's older son drove to her house in his car, Jeanne was being driven home separately by her younger son. As he was driving her home, with just the two of them in his car, he told her that even though, under inheritance laws, he was entitled to a part of his father's estate, his father would have wanted Jeanne to have a comfortable life. He told Jeanne that she had always been a loving mother, and, therefore, he was turning over his entire share of the estate to her. He expected his brother to do the same because he was sure that his brother felt the same way about her.

The three of them met at Jeanne's house. When they later sat down for dinner, Jeanne's younger son repeated his wish for their mother to receive the entire estate. Surprisingly, his older brother hotly rejected that suggestion, and said that as far as he was concerned, he was entitled to what the law provided to him as a son. He went on to say that he intended to get everything he was entitled to, and, furthermore, he expected to get his share as soon as the law allowed. He also said that he was going into the house to take his share of what he felt Dad had left for him and would take his share of the gold coins and silverware. He also said to his brother that he should mind his own business.

The brothers could not have had more differing attitudes. One son wanted to protect Mom's financial position, and the other son wanted his share of Dad's money and household things. The friction between them could not be resolved by Mom or by any other family member. Before long, they stopped talking to one another. After that, Jeanne's younger son told her that he wanted nothing to do with his greedy, selfish brother. He said that he was so upset with his brother that he would only visit Mom when he knew that his brother wasn't going to be in the house.

Jeanne said that she loved both of her sons and understood the way each of them felt. Her older son felt he was doing what he was entitled to do, and her younger son felt that he was doing what he ought to do. She then told us what she expected to happen on the next Mother's Day. She said that the first part of Mother's Day would be for one son, and the rest would be for the other. She decided to do this because her younger son had already told her that next Mother's Day, she should call him to come over as soon as his brother leaves the house. She sobbed, "I'll never see my two children together again, and the next time my boys will be together will probably be at my funeral."

35. MY BROTHER THREW IT ALL AWAY

A caller to a radio show, one of two brothers, told us the following story, voicing the hope that he was not going to sound like a selfish person.

He said that he was the saver in the family and his brother had always been the spender. In the caller's own words, "nothing was too good for my brother. He always had a live-for-today attitude." When their dad passed away, the two brothers shared his estate, worth well over three million dollars. The caller used part of his share of the inheritance to pay off his mortgage. He invested the balance for his retirement.

On the other hand, the caller said that his brother sold the house he was living in and moved into a large, expensive home. Less than six months had passed since their father died, when the caller visited his brother's new home. In the driveway he could see his brother's two brand new cars. His brother bragged to him that he was about to buy a new condominium in Florida, and that his wife had booked an appointment to get some very expensive cosmetic surgery. The caller's tone on the air sounded somewhat sarcastic at this point, when he said, "like they really needed all of this."

If that was bad enough, his brother and sister-in-law also bragged to him about the investments they had made. They laughed at the caller for being so conservative in the investments he chose. His brother and sister had placed the majority of their share of the inheritance in high-risk investments. They justified their choice by telling the caller that they would be very rich "once things go our way." They added their own advice to this, saying to the caller, in their own words, "Life is full of risks. Your way of investing is too timid. What are you afraid of?"

The caller said that he had vivid memories of his brother and sister-in-law talking to him this way, because over the next year, all he seemed to hear from them were their lectures on how to get rich. "We're making some real money from what Dad left us," they would repeat over and over.

The good times did not last very much longer, though, for the caller's brother and sister-in-law. One night, the caller got a desperate call from his brother, begging for money. His brother complained that most of his investments were lost in the market downturn, and now he had no money to pay the mortgage on his new house. He had no money left to maintain his Florida condominium. His car payments and his other bills were overwhelming him. His salary was not enough to cover all of these expenses. He pleaded with our caller for help. In the words quoted by the caller, his brother said, "The money you inherited came from OUR father and he would have wanted you to help me when I needed it. A brother should help a brother when he is down."

The caller said that his brother's plea for help tore him apart. On one hand, he had always been there for his brother, but on the other hand, he felt that his brother's spending habits had ruined him. Our caller believed very strongly that once he opened the door and bailed out his brother, the rest of their parents' life savings would just flow into a bottomless pit.

After wrestling with this troubling decision, the caller said that this time, he had to say "no" to his brother because he had blown his half of the inheritance. The caller spoke of how this inherited money represented years and years of Dad's hard work, and his brother had just thrown the money away on extravagance in less than two years.

The caller's last words were, "I feel really bad for my brother, and all of this really bothers me. But, I know Dad would feel that I did the right thing."

36. A FEW SECONDS IN A LIFE (HOW FAST LIFE CAN CHANGE)

A couple had come to our office to make their wills. The husband told me that he had just turned 65. He said that because of his severe physical disabilities, he didn't know what he would do without his wife. As he was telling me this, I saw his wife stabilize him as he removed his hands from his walker and prepared to sit down in a chair in our boardroom. The body language of his wife made it clear to me that she was very much in love with him.

Almost without hesitation, each of them told me that they were leaving everything they owned to one another. They wanted each other appointed as executor, with their friend as a back-up. They had no children, and as a result, when both of them were gone, they wanted their estates to be left to a charity.

However, my dialogue with this couple went beyond the financial aspect of their lives, and I found myself engaged in a very personal and emotional discussion with them. In the course of that discussion, they both bared their souls to me.

The husband spoke of his frustration in being unable to provide a better life for the woman he loved so much. He described her to me as his angel, as he looked into her eyes. He said to me, even as his eyes were still on her, that it pained him to know the fulfilment he was unable to give to her, because of his physical disabilities.

She responded that she loved him from the first moment she saw him, and she married him for who he was, not for his legs.

Speaking on such an intensely personal level, it did not take very long for the husband to talk about the cause of his physical grief. "I wasn't born like this. I was once strong and healthy."

The husband shifted his gaze to me, looked out the window, and then back at me. He said that he would give everything he had and more, if only he could take back the few seconds that changed the entire course of his life.

He said that hardly a day goes by without this crossing his mind.

He said that he and his family lived in the lower apartment of a duplex. Duplexes in his city were built so that both the lower apartment and the upper one had balconies facing the backyard. You could go up the back stairs and go to either the lower balcony or the upper one. In the winter time, one of the things he liked to do in his youth was to jump off the lower balcony into the snow in the backyard. When he woke up one morning during the early winter of 1954, he never thought that something would happen that day that would change his life forever. As he spoke, his facial expression began to change, and I could feel that he was tensing up. I could tell that what he was about to say was going to bring some strong emotions to the surface. He said, "When you wake up each morning, you don't think that this will be the day that your life will be forever changed."

He then described those few seconds which had such an impact on the rest of his life. He wanted to show off with a high dive into the snow from the upper balcony of his mother's house. He had done this from the lower balcony too many times to count, but he had never attempted the jump from the upper balcony.

He remembered how his mother had warned him what could happen to him if he took chances like that. He usually listened to what his mother had to say. All he remembers, though, is that in a few seconds of weakness, he wanted to impress the girl who lived up the street, and that is why he did the high dive from the upper balcony. That high dive disabled him for life.

37. BUT DAD PROMISED ME

Iris said that Dad always called her his "gift from Heaven." He became chronically ill a few years after her Mom passed away, and as his health began to deteriorate, Iris moved into his condominium to be with him. Her two brothers were both married, and had their own homes. Iris was single. When Dad passed away, Iris was still living in Dad's condominium.

When it came time to distribute Dad's estate, Iris expected, based on what Dad had told her, that his will would leave the condo to her, and that the estate would be split equally between Iris and her two brothers. However, her two brothers, who were the executors of Dad's estate, pointed out to Iris that Dad's will said nothing about leaving her the condo. In fact, it specifically split his whole estate three ways. They said that if Dad had intended Iris to get the condo, his will would have spelled that out. They also said that the first they ever heard about Iris supposedly getting the condo, was from Iris herself, and that was only after Dad had passed away. They had not heard anything about this when Dad was alive. Iris responded to them by saying that Dad was not well enough to redo his will, and if he had been well enough, he would have redone his will to leave her the condo.

The arguments between Iris and her brothers went back and forth. She said that she had been a very loyal caregiver to Dad and had spent over a year of her life devoting herself to his needs at a time when he needed her most.

Her brothers countered that after all, Iris was single, without any other commitments, and besides that, she enjoyed over a year of free rent living with Dad. Furthermore, her brothers were adamant that if Dad had wanted her to have something, he would have said so to them, and would have put it in his will. However, Dad never said anything about this to either of them. Iris's brothers were highly suspicious about the fact that the condo issue suddenly came up after Dad was gone. They told Iris that if Dad had mentioned to either of them, even once, that he wanted Iris to get the condo, then they would have respected his wishes. On Dad's word alone, they would have handed the condo to Iris.

Iris replied that Dad had called her into his room before he died and told her that he wanted to reward her devotion by leaving the condo to her. The fact was, though, that her brothers were never called into that room.

In the end, her brothers felt that Iris was fabricating a story in order to get the condo. Iris was insulted by the fact that her brothers would not take her word, and she found it offensive that they were accusing her of lying to them. Despite these negative feelings, the two brothers allowed Iris to live in the condo, paying rent to the estate. They did agree that the condo would not be sold, as long as she kept paying the rent. This resolved the legal problem, but from that point onward, her relationship with her brothers was strictly business. Iris was a tenant in her Dad's condo. She paid her rent and as far as she was concerned, she no longer had brothers.

38. WHO'S STUPID NOW?

Tobias graduated with a business degree from a highly respected university. He had done well, ranking near the top of his class. After graduation, he became an investment advisor in a major bank. His parents, Ethel and Harvey, had been fairly well off, but during the time that Tobias was still attending university studies, they lost almost everything they had on a very speculative and ill-timed real estate investment. As Tobias came to learn of the disastrous results of their investment, he felt anger because they never asked him for his input. In fact, Tobias became so frustrated by the resulting losses for the whole family, that he completely lost respect for his parents. He felt that there was no excuse for their gambling away his inheritance.

Ethel and Harvey tried to explain to Tobias that they had worked hard for decades and had always been conservative in what they chose to invest in. They told him that this one real estate deal looked like a sure thing and was too good to pass up. They explained that, in fact, the investment went bad because their timing was bad. Had the same transaction taken place six months later, they would have made a huge profit instead of suffering a devastating loss.

Tobias was not impressed by what his parents had to tell him. He adopted such a frigid attitude towards them that when he eventually had his own children, he poisoned their minds toward Ethel and Harvey. Tobias made no secret of how he felt about his parents.

If there happened to be a family function which involved Tobias and his parents, Tobias would usually find a way to degrade his parents, calling them "backward," "stupid," "ignorant," and even worse terms than that. Tobias had no hesitation in embarrassing his parents in front of other family members and even strangers.

Except for these sporadic family gatherings, the years otherwise passed in hostile silence. Ethel and Harvey were perfectly aware of how Tobias looked down at them.

However, because Tobias kept the communications with his parents to a bare minimum, he had no way of knowing that his parents continued their hard work, invested wisely and made back all of their losses and much more.

When Ethel and Harvey decided to update their wills, they left their entire estates to one another. Their wills also provided that when both of them were to pass away, the only person who would inherit from them was their other child, Diane. Tobias was cut out of their wills.

After they had signed their wills, Ethel and Harvey gave a package to Diane in order that she have the best protection against any legal challenge that Tobias might bring to attack their wills, after they pass away. There were a number of documents in their package, including true copies of the signed wills, records of what they owned, and the business card of the lawyer who held the originals of their wills. They also inserted a signed letter from their doctor which attested to the fact that both Ethel and Harvey had full mental capacity at the time of signing their wills. As well, they included a signed letter which set out, in writing, their reasons for cutting their son out of their wills. Ethel and Harvey explained that these were all designed to shield Diane from her brother, after they had passed away. They also gave Diane a sealed envelope, addressed to Tobias, for Diane to mail to him after they were gone. The sealed envelope contained another copy of their letter setting out their reasons for cutting Tobias out of their wills.

In their letter, Ethel and Harvey told Tobias in no uncertain terms, how he insulted them, hurt them, embarrassed them in front of family and strangers, and had even turned his own children against them. They went on to say that Tobias had never believed in them, that his business degree had gone to his head, and that he should be ashamed of himself for disrespecting them as he did for so many years, and for repeatedly calling them stupid people. They also explained that because of Tobias's hurtful attitude, their entire estates were being left to his sister, Diane. The last line on the letter to Tobias read, "We made a lot more money than we lost. You're not getting any of it. Who's the stupid one now?"

39. BUT THEY ARE MY PARENTS

This story is about two cousins, Bill and Fred, who for most of their lives were very close. Their relationship formed over many decades, but it was destroyed in less than fifteen minutes because of certain words that were spoken. What Bill may have meant to say to Fred, in a spirit of friendship and concern, was taken by Fred as inconsiderate, hurtful, and insulting.

Every Thursday night, for years, they would meet at a quiet restaurant for an hour or so to share a meal and a beer, and to talk about matters of family, business, sports, and whatever else crossed their minds.

One Thursday evening, Fred, who was an only child, happened to be speaking about his parents, who were in their eighties and in failing health. Both of Fred's parents were very sick, with heart conditions. In addition, Fred's mother had serious osteoporosis. Fred's father had arthritis so painful that he could barely walk, and when he did so, it was with a walker. Both parents had given up driving, and relied heavily on Fred's caregiving.

Fred was a postal worker. He made a decent salary, but the majority of what he earned was being spent on his parents. Fred bought a special bed for his father. He paid for in-home nursing care, bought his parents therapeutic aids, and since they could not get out, he also bought them a home entertainment system.

Fred felt that he had an obligation to help his parents because when he was younger, they did so much for him, and he was always their first priority.

Now that his parents needed his help, they were his first priority, and he would do whatever he had to in order to make their lives better.

However, this meant that Fred needed to watch his own expenses. Watching his own expenses meant cutting back on his entertainment and travel. As a result, Fred's girlfriend was beginning to get upset over the fact that Fred's parents were the priority in his life. Fred, however, was very close to his parents, and it was important to him that they lived their lives in the most comfortable way possible, in their condominium.

Bill was attentive to Fred's description of the way he was helping his parents, but as Fred's close friend and cousin, he wanted to raise a sensitive subject with Fred.

Bill told Fred that if he kept devoting most of his time and money to his parents, he would ruin his own life, and probably lose his girlfriend. If Fred kept on as he was, Bill felt that Fred might bankrupt himself and certainly would have little money left for his own old age. As a result of all of these concerns, Bill told Fred that he should seriously consider placing his parents on a list for a nursing home. He told Fred to move on with his life before it was too late. Bill said that Fred's parents were in their eighties, and would understand that a nursing home would give them better care than they had at home.

Fred was absolutely shocked at his cousin's attitude. He told Bill that both of his parents had voiced their fears of living in a nursing home. They wanted to live in their own home for as long as possible. Fred said that he had vowed to his parents that he would protect them, and follow their wishes. He would not let them down.

Bill repeated his point over and over again, that Fred's parents ought to sell their condominium and move to a nursing home, and improve all of their lives. Fred kept making his point, that putting his parents in a nursing home was not the right thing to do. Bill kept telling Fred that he was wrong. The discussion turned argumentative as they raised their voices to each other.

Fred told Bill that he was callous, inhuman, and was ignorant of how a real relationship should be between parent and child. Bill said that Fred was being taken advantage of and used by his parents, and was just too blind to see it. Fred said to Bill that this was none of his business, and he hoped Bill's children would treat him as shabbily when the time came that Bill would need their help. Bill became sarcastic, calling Fred a baby who never grew up. Fred retorted that his parents had always been there for him, and if the situation had been reversed, his parents would never think of letting him down, the way

Bill now wanted Fred to let them down. And with that, Fred had enough. He pulled $20 out of his wallet, slammed it down on the table, and left without another word. That was the last Thursday the two cousins ever spent together.

40. DAD HELPED HER BEHIND MY BACK

Reg had this story to tell.

When his Mom and Dad separated, he moved in with his Dad, and his only sister, Beth, went to live with Mom. Once Reg started living with Dad, he stopped all communications with Mom and Beth. Reg blamed them for causing the separation and blamed them for all of Dad's stress and aggravation.

Several months after the separation agreement was finalized, Dad showed Reg the new will that his lawyer prepared. Reg was the executor and sole beneficiary under this will. His father had cut Beth out of his new will. Reg remembers Dad telling him, "She's my daughter but she's a lazy good for nothing."

For the next several years, Reg was very close to Dad. He was devastated when Dad suddenly had a massive heart attack and died. Reg met Beth for the first time in years at Dad's funeral. All Beth had to say to Reg was to ask him, "Did Dad leave a will?" Reg had a one-line answer for his sister, "Yes, he made a will and there is nothing in it for you."

A number of weeks after Reg began to work on Dad's estate, he was surprised to receive a package from a lawyer who was unknown to Reg. He was shocked when he opened the package and found that it had been sent by a lawyer acting on behalf of his sister, Beth.

Beth's lawyer sent Reg a medical report showing that Beth was suffering from severe depression and could not work. He also sent Reg photocopied money orders and bank drafts totalling tens of thousands of dollars, stretching back for years, sent to Beth by Dad, right up to the month before he died. The contents of the package included a cover letter from Beth's lawyer. It stated that although Beth was cut out of the will and was too old to get child support, she was still going to make a claim as a dependant of her father's estate. The lawyer's letter went on to explain the reasoning behind this claim. He explained that for many years, Beth's father was supporting her on an ongoing basis for the necessities of her life. Beth's lawyer wrote that Beth would win at court as a dependant, because the court would see that her father had been supporting her financially for years. The photocopies of the money orders and the bank drafts in the package were evidence of such support. She needed this money for food, for rent, for her medications, her transportation, and anything else that her condition demanded. Furthermore, the lawyer's letter stated that from the medical information in his hands, unless her condition improved, her dependency would be permanent. The lawyer's letter went on to demand that no funds in the estate be touched until his client's claim is resolved.

Reg could not believe that his father's estate was now going to be contested. It was even more shocking to Reg that his father could give so much money to his sister for so long without even a hint to Reg that any of this was happening. When Reg showed all of this to his own lawyer, the bad news from his lawyer was that he did not have much of a defence. It made Reg sick to see his sister trying to drain Dad's estate dry. To put it in Reg's own words, "She's not sick; she's as healthy as I am. She doesn't want to work, and now she just wants to live off my father's hard work."

The problem for Reg was that no matter which way he turned, there was going to be little or nothing left for him from Dad's estate. If he fought Beth, he was probably going to throw good money after bad on what his lawyer felt was a losing case. If he didn't fight her, he would be saddled with the obligation to finance the future of a sister who didn't have the time of day for him or Dad.

41. JOINT OWNERSHIP: I SHOULD NEVER HAVE DONE IT

A caller to a radio call-in show told us about a financial disaster she endured due to being given the wrong advice. This was her story.

The caller's major asset was her home. Her husband had died a few years before, leaving the home to her. She listened to the advice of a friend who told her to put the home in joint names with her son, so that her son could avoid having to probate her will when she died.

With that in mind, she went to a lawyer to arrange the paperwork to do this, but the lawyer advised her to think twice about it. The lawyer told her that it would be risky to put her son on the title in case something negative happened to her son. The examples the lawyer gave her were bankruptcy and divorce.

The caller thanked the lawyer for advising her to be cautious, but she felt that she had nothing to worry about when it came to her son's finances or his marriage. She said that her objective was to avoid probate. She retained another lawyer to transfer half of the interest in her home, to her son.

About a year later, a reversal of fortune in her son's business destroyed it and exposed him to large personal debts. The very scenario that the first lawyer had cautioned her about suddenly became reality. Worse yet, her son declared personal bankruptcy. She was worried sick about what would happen to her home. She could not sleep at night. She had to be treated by her doctor for her severe stress, worrying about losing her home.

Before long, she received a letter from the lawyer who acted for her son's trustee in bankruptcy. The letter explained that the trustee now owned her son's half of the home because of the bankruptcy. She was very upset that the trustee demanded payment for his half interest in the home. The letter stated that she could buy the half of the home that was now owned by the trustee. If not, she was warned that he could force the sale of the entire home, and would then split the proceeds with her. This turned her stress into anger at her son. She was also angry at her friend who gave her the foolish advice to put her home in joint names with her son. She was also angry at herself for rejecting the proper advice from the first attorney. She told us that she no longer talks to her son or to that friend any more.

The caller said that now she cannot reverse the destruction of her financial security. She said that the least she could do was to alert the public to the dangers of giving up control over something that belongs to you. Her last comment was, "Don't be naïve like me."

42. A FAMILY TREE WITH MISSING BRANCHES

During a flight home from my vacation, I got involved in a discussion with a young man sitting beside me. Bill was a law student, and when the subject of wills and inheritance battles came up, I mentioned that I was co-author of two books on the subject. This prompted Bill to talk about his own family. He said that before getting into the stories he wanted to tell, he wanted to make one point. As Bill put it, "because too many branches of our family tree have been cut off, my brother and I vowed never to let ourselves fall into the same trap as our relatives did." This is the rest of what Bill had to say.

Bill's great-grandfather had vast landholdings. According to the stories that were handed down to Bill, his great-grandfather felt that a woman's role was that of homemaker. He felt that women were to look after running the household, and that money and property were to be dealt with by men. His great-grandfather ultimately prepared a will which left his vast landholdings to his son (Bill's grandmother's brother). This had the effect of cutting Bill's grandmother out of the vast holdings of her father's estate.

Bill appeared to have a strong grasp of his family history. He continued with the sad narrative of how his grandmother pleaded with her brother to share some of the vast wealth he inherited from their father, and how her pleas fell upon the deaf ears of her brother. As a result of that, his grandmother and her descendants became estranged from her wealthy brother and his descendants.

These wealthy descendants had nothing to do with Bill or his family, and similarly, Bill never looked upon them as part of what Bill described as "his family."

Bill's parents had always cautioned him and his brother never to trust the relatives from the wealthy side of the family. His parents looked upon those people as "strangers who are up to their necks in greed."

Bill made a point of saying that if only his grandmother had received even a small fraction of the inheritance left to her brother, he and his family would have all been millionaires today, and that his family would have avoided many financial struggles.

Bill's grandmother lived through very difficult years, where money was scarce and poverty was a constant threat. She became a widow early in her hard life, just after her two daughters were born. One of those girls was Bill's mother. The other was Bill's Aunt Anne.

Bill told of how his grandmother, his Mom, and his Aunt Anne lived a frugal existence. They all worked seven days a week in their small store. The business ruled their lives. Over time, with hard work and perseverance, the business made some money, and the family began to emerge from their hard life. During these years, Bill's mother and his Aunt Anne each met their husbands. Bill's Mom married his Dad, and his Aunt Anne married his Uncle Charles. Bill's grandmother worked in the store until the day she passed away.

This ended part one of Bill's story. Sadly, the fragmenting of his family did not end there. He continued with part two.

Bill's Uncle Charles was the next person who ripped away another branch of his family tree. Bill described Uncle Charles as a liar and a troublemaker who instigated a new round of friction and antagonism in his family.

Uncle Charles seemed to enjoy demeaning Bill's mother. Their relationship was strained, almost from the first time they ever met.

In addition, there was a side to Uncle Charles that only came out after Bill's grandmother died. Uncle Charles was a manipulative person and he had a strong influence on Aunt Anne, who was a mild-mannered woman. His ability to influence his wife eventually led to a bitter fight between Bill's Mom and his Aunt Anne.

Bill felt that if he heard twenty lies from Uncle Charles about his Mom, there must have been sixty more that he never heard. For example, Bill spoke of how his Aunt Anne believed that Bill's Mom didn't work nearly as long or as hard in the store as she did. Bill had no doubt in his mind where that came from. He described how Uncle Charles would poison her mind against his Mom, and he reeled off many more examples of the lies and the false accusations made about his Mom. However, Bill described the final straw that broke the camel's back, permanently tearing apart his Mom and his Aunt Anne. Uncle Charles falsely accused Bill's mother of stealing one of the investments made by their business.

Uncle Charles found an investment certificate which should have been recorded in the name of the business. However, the certificate was recorded by the bank as being in the name of Bill's Mom. Uncle Charles immediately called Bill's Mom a crook. Bill's Mom had overlooked many of Charles's false accusations in the past, but there was no way that she would tolerate being called a thief. She knew that what Charles was complaining about must have been some error because she knew nothing about any bank certificate in her name.

She called her sister, Anne, to tell her that she should put her husband in his place. Anne refused, saying that she believed every word her husband had to say about the bank certificate. She said,

"My husband thinks that you stole money from our company, and I believe him. I think you are a liar and a cheat. Charles was always right about you." Bill's Mom was heartbroken from losing her sister's trust. A lifetime of trust between the two sisters now seemed to be thrown away. To make matters worse, Uncle Charles then hired a lawyer and a forensic investigator to prove this alleged theft. What came out of months of investigation was that the bank had made an honest error and they wrote a letter of apology to both Bill's mother and to Bill's aunt, admitting the bank's error.

This proved beyond any doubt that there never had been any theft by Bill's mother. But by this time, there was also no relationship left between the two sisters.

Since that time, Bill did not see or speak to his uncle, his aunt, or any of their children. When he happened to pass his aunt on the street, he turned his head away from her. They passed each other in cold silence. Sadly, the family tree lost another limb, and probably forever.

Bill then told me about his own relationship with his brother, and how he and his brother loved one another. Each of them was best friend and confidante to the other. They would do anything for each other. Bill said that he and his brother were determined to protect this treasured relationship from the tragic events that had haunted two generations of his family, so far. He vowed that nothing and nobody would ever drive him and his brother apart.

At that point, Bill told me about the written agreement that he and his brother signed, in order to preserve and protect their relationship with one another. They did not want to repeat the mistakes made in previous generations.

Shortly stated, the agreement provided that no matter what their mother's will said, and no matter what property was held in any joint account between either of them and their mother, everything would always be equally split between them. They also provided that to the best of their ability, they would not include their spouses in any business dealings between them. He ended by saying that his family tree had lost its last limb.

43. THE APPARENT MILLIONAIRE

You know the old expression "all that glitters is not gold." If anyone has been witness to the truth of this saying, it is Mary, who told us her story at a financial planning seminar in which we were participants, together with insurance brokers and other professionals.

After Mary had lost her husband Lionel, she discovered that she was named as executor in his will. At first glance, it appeared to her that she was simply going to distribute his large estate between herself and the two adult sons from Lionel's first marriage. The assets in the estate consisted of several apartment buildings, luxury cars, expensive jewellery, and two country homes.

She had lived with Lionel in a magnificent lakefront home.

Lionel had divorced his first wife because he had fallen in love with Mary, and ultimately married her. Mary felt that Lionel's sons had never forgiven her for taking their father away from their mother.

Lionel's will left one-third of the estate to her, and two-thirds to his sons.

Lionel's sons, according to Mary, had lived their version of their late father's lavish lifestyle. One son drove a Porsche, the other, a Ferrari. Mary was aware, from what Lionel had told her, that he had been paying his sons excessive salaries from the family management company for years.

Mary was anxious for Lionel's estate to be finalized. She wanted her step-sons out of her life.

Lionel's sons were desperate to get their hands on the majority of the estate. From what Mary had told us, each of her step-sons had incurred a mountain of debt, and they needed their share of the estate to clear it.

The first steps in the administration of Lionel's estate were to obtain appraisals, valuations, and tax opinions in order to determine just how large his estate was.

Almost immediately after Lionel passed away, the bitterness between Mary and her step-sons translated into correspondence between lawyers. Lionel's sons had begun to attack Mary's role as executor. Their lawyer demanded that Mary prepare accounts for them to review, and he accused Mary of deliberately dragging her feet. The lawyer also made it clear that his clients did not trust Mary to administer this estate, given its expected size and the fact that his clients had the majority interest in it.

Meanwhile, as all this was happening, the accountant and the valuator were working on their reports. After a few weeks, both reports were completed. The reports contained some unpleasant surprises. Mary was shocked when she read their findings.

The reports described how all of the apartment buildings and the two country homes were mortgaged to the hilt. Beyond that, Lionel had dealt with the apartment buildings in the worst imaginable way from an income tax point of view. Year after year, against the advice of his accountant, he had taken write-offs beyond the maximum allowable by law, and it was only by sheer luck that he had never been audited.

Put simply, the estate owed serious money to the government, which had a major claim over whatever Lionel had left. All of Lionel's assets taken together, including his heavily mortgaged real estate, were insufficient to satisfy the debts and taxes.

Lionel had kept all of the detail of his financial affairs so hidden from Mary that even in relating this story to us long after the events occurred, Mary said that she never got over the shock that she felt when she came face-to-face with the financial wreckage that she inherited from her late husband.

She said that she was not the only one who was in a state of disbelief. Her step-sons were furious with her, accusing Mary of living "the lifestyle of a queen" while driving her husband to the poorhouse. They had started a vicious lawsuit against her. Surprisingly, it ended after a few months, when her step-sons suddenly discontinued their proceedings against her. No reason was given, but Mary assumed that her step-sons had run out of money for their lawyer. She described the irony in all of this because in the end, if that was the case, it was Lionel who had left both her and her step-sons in such weak financial positions that neither of them could afford to fight the other. Mary was facing an uncertain financial future.

Lionel had mortgaged to raise his own lifestyle, and left behind a painful reality for his heirs, which bore no resemblance to the illusions that he created during his life. As Mary went back to take her seat to listen to the next speaker, her parting words were "after all is said and done, there was nothing for me to inherit and nothing for Lionel's sons either."

44. IF ONLY DAD HAD THOUGHT ABOUT THE FUTURE

This story is about a father who could not care less about the future and who took money for granted. His attitude would turn out to have very negative effects upon his family after he passed away.

Dad always felt that "things would work themselves out." As a result, his earnings were devoted to whatever pleased him. He drove a very expensive convertible. He lived in a beautiful home and did not mind paying a large mortgage payment every month. Dad took Mom on expensive vacations to exotic places in Asia, and to resorts in the Caribbean and in Europe at least twice a year. He wanted Mom to look after their home and the children, so Mom never had a job and never made any money of her own.

From time to time Mom suggested that they "invest for the future." Dad wouldn't listen. When he impulsively wanted to sell the family home just before the real estate boom of the 1970's, Mom felt that Dad was making a mistake, but she could not change his mind. So she went along with him. As a result, they sold their home just before the price of real estate began to skyrocket. Dad now had fresh money to continue buying whatever pleased him. But now Mom and Dad were renting instead of owning. Dad's "live for today" attitude planted the seeds for the rest of this story.

Mom and Dad had three children. Bernard, the eldest, grew up to be a hard-working and successful professional. He was not by any means wealthy, but he lived by the lessons he learned from Dad's errors. He was a saver. He and his family lived a modest life.

Erin, their only daughter, was also hard-working. Just like her brother Bernard, she also was a saver and lived modestly.

The middle child, Simon, was a businessman. He loved to brag about himself, to Bernard and Erin. For years, they heard about his cars, his exotic travels, and the expensive universities in far-off places where he sent his children. They heard of his mingling with important people in the world of entertainment and politics. They did not know exactly how wealthy Simon was, but they both felt that his wealth was substantial.

After Dad passed away, the family seemed to be closely knit. Mom continued to live in her apartment, and Bernard, Erin, and Simon all got along reasonably well.

When Mom turned 90, Simon decided that Mom had to move to a decent retirement home. He persuaded Bernard and Erin that this was the right time for her to move. Mom went along with his suggestion. All three children loved Mom and wanted her to be well looked after. Erin found a very decent retirement home that would cost Mom about $3,000 per month. However, Simon said that only the very best was good enough for Mom, and he pushed for a luxurious residence for Mom that cost twice as much per month. Simon was insistent on moving Mom to the more expensive residence, no matter the cost. He was resolute, and neither Erin nor Bernard could change his mind.

It was at that point, that Mom signed the lease, and, for the first time, revealed her finances to her kids. Dad had left some savings, but no investments. His estate was minimal. Mom could afford at best $1,000 per month. The question then arose, as to who would pay for the rest? Simon, who had been pushing this so hard, thought that Mom was far better off financially than she really was.

There was a need for someone to pay the remaining $5,000 per month for the retirement home lease, on a permanent basis. Suddenly, Simon begged for a "break" from his other two siblings.

He confessed to them that he had been living beyond his means. He had been running up credit card debt for a long time. He mortgaged his home and then re-mortgaged it in order to pay down the credit card debt. He admitted that it was wrong to brag to his own brother and sister. Now he was pleading with them to pick up most of the financial burden for Mom's retirement home. Simon had to backtrack on his demand for the expensive residence and now wanted Mom to go to the less expensive one that Erin had originally found. Erin was now forced to beg for Mom's release from the lease for the expensive residence and was also forced to go back to the first, less expensive one, to see if they still had a place for Mom. There was anxiety in the family while they all waited to see if Erin would meet with success on both matters.

Fortunately, Erin was able to get the legal release from the expensive residence, and to squeeze Mom into the last remaining space in the first retirement home. She was very upset that Simon had put her to the trouble of begging twice in order to end up with the arrangements she had made for Mom in the first place, before Simon had stuck his nose into this matter.

Baring his soul to his siblings was not only damaging to Simon's ego, but also to his marriage. Erin and Bernard agreed to pick up more than their fair share of the monthly rent for Mom, but this was for a price. They demanded that Simon devote all of the effort necessary to move Mom from her apartment to the retirement residence. Simon had a hard time explaining to his wife that the two of them would now have to devote their entire vacation time to working out Mom's move. In turn, Simon's wife was embarrassed because she would have to cancel the vacation plans they had made with their friends, and she was upset at Simon for this last-minute change.

Another link in this ready-to-break chain was the financial accommodation made to Simon by Bernard and Erin which ended up being a greater financial burden on the two of them than they could have ever imagined. Now each of them had to explain to their spouses why their family had to shoulder more of the monthly burden than Simon's family did.

This created a tension between the three families, which could most likely be traced right back to Dad's cavalier attitude toward money and his failure to consider the following important question: "What will happen to my wife if I pass away and she needs to be cared for?"

45. PROTECTING MY LITTLE GIRL

Yvonne, a 40-year-old widow, was taken by surprise by her doctor's diagnosis. Her doctor confirmed that she had a terminal illness and that she only had about three to six months to live. She felt that she was too young to die, especially because her only daughter, Emily, was only eight years old.

For five years, Yvonne had lived with her boyfriend, Eugene. They were going to get married someday. Now, Yvonne knew that the wedding day would never come.

She came to speak to me about two weeks after her diagnosis. She was very concerned about Emily and wanted to make her will so that Emily would have the best protection possible.

An important first step in making her will was for me to ask Yvonne about a guardian for little Emily. I carefully asked her, "Whom do you want to name in your will as Emily's guardian? As you know, this is who you would select to raise Emily after you're gone." She began to sob and said, "Two months ago, we were celebrating Emily's eighth birthday party. I could never have imagined that something like this would happen to me." She said that she had trouble thinking this through because it all happened so fast. She was very uncertain about whether she should name her sister or her mother. Her sister was very close to her, but had three of her own children, and Yvonne was worried that the added weight of another child might burden her sister financially. As well, Yvonne was worried about whether Emily would get enough attention from her sister. On the other hand, Yvonne's mother was seventy years old, and while she was capable and loving, Yvonne was worried about how long her mother would be up to taking care of a young girl like Emily.

Yvonne asked me to draft the will leaving the name of the guardian blank, and said she would call me during the week to let me know who she would name. She called three times, naming her sister the first time, then changing it to her mother, then back to her sister, and that is how the draft of the will ended up, in preparation for her appointment the following week.

I will never forget that appointment. Yvonne came to the office with her boyfriend Eugene and her daughter Emily. Yvonne introduced me to both of them. Emily was carrying magic markers and a paint-by-numbers book. Eugene was sombre, respectful, and very quiet. He sat with Emily in the waiting room while Yvonne came into the boardroom with me so that she could review the will before she signed it.

As she sat at the boardroom table, she began to cry. "Who would know the special stories Emily loves? They are the ones we made up together. Who would know the special way I brush her hair, or the games we play after supper?" She went on and then, sobbing, said she couldn't name her sister as guardian. No way. Emily would not get enough attention. Yvonne was now out of breath, and crying so much that she needed more tissue.

As I went out to get a box of tissue for her, I could still hear her crying. So could Emily and Eugene. Emily looked up from her paint-by-numbers book, and asked Eugene, "What's wrong with Mommy?" Eugene patted her hand and told her he would straighten everything out. He walked into the boardroom with me, and Yvonne hugged him and cried, "I don't know what to do! I don't know what to do!" Suddenly Yvonne became a little girl and just looked at Eugene. I had to explain to Eugene what Yvonne's dilemma was. I don't think the words were out of my mouth for twenty seconds, when Eugene said, "Yvonne, name me. Emily is part of my love for you. I will never let you down, and as long as I live, I will never let her down."

Through her tears, Yvonne told Eugene that she had never wanted to chain him to anything after she was gone. That is why she didn't initially name him as guardian. But Eugene repeated that Emily had been an important part of his own life. He looked upon her as his own daughter, and that the life he wanted was a life that included Emily. Yvonne then cried uncontrollably. Through her tears, she said, "I love you Gene and I always will. I promise that I will watch over the two of you forever."

It took a few minutes for Yvonne to regain her composure, and I was trying to keep mine. Yvonne nodded to me to finalize the will, naming Eugene as Emily's guardian.

Eugene left the boardroom when the final version of the will was brought in for signing. When Yvonne signed it in front of the witness and me, her only words were, "Now, I can pass away in peace, knowing that my daughter is in loving hands."

She then asked me to sit with her for a few minutes, while she wiped the tears from her eyes and her face. She held a small mirror, and her hand shook a bit as she did her best to apply some makeup. She did not want Emily to see that she had still been crying.

As I walked her out to the waiting room, Emily reached for her mother's hand, and that is how mother and daughter walked out the front door. Eugene walked behind them. That was the last time I ever saw them. Although many years have passed since then, every time I see a mother and a young daughter walking hand-in-hand, I think of Yvonne, and the love she left for Emily.

46. CAUGHT BETWEEN MY WIFE AND MY SISTER

Gerald wished that he could erase just one evening from his life.

As far as Gerald had been aware, the settlement of Dad's estate was routine and amicable. Both before and after Dad passed away, every two or three weeks, his only sister, Ramona, would invite Gerald and his wife to her home, or Gerald and his wife would invite Ramona and her husband to come over to their home.

About a year after Dad died, Gerald and his wife were visiting Ramona and her husband. After dinner, they all happened to be watching a TV show about a courtroom battle over an estate. As they watched, something led Ramona to exclaim, "I should have hired a lawyer when Dad died. I don't think that I got what I should have."

At first, Gerald let the comment pass, even though he felt it was offensive. He thought it was simply an impulsive reaction of his sister.

However, she repeated this comment again during the commercial break, and then went on to add that Gerald should have told her to get advice from an independent lawyer, that he ripped her off, and that he pushed her into accepting her share of the estate.

Gerald then responded, "C'mon Sis, stop." Ramona would not stop and accused him of totally taking advantage of her at the time. Gerald denied this, saying he did nothing of the sort, and that the estate was distributed equally and fairly. Gerald told her that he didn't even take a dime of compensation for his work as executor of Dad's estate.

At this point, Gerald's wife came to his defence and yelled at Ramona, "You're calling my husband a thief and that is disgusting. He would never do anything to hurt you." Ramona shouted back, "It's none of your **** business; you're just my sister-in-law; you're not my relative; and what goes on between me and my brother doesn't concern you."

The two women continued to yell and swear at one another to the point where it looked like there might be violence. Gerald tried, without success, to put himself between the two women who were now pushing at one another. He was concerned at this point that someone outside on the street might hear all of this and call the police. Suddenly, Gerald's wife grabbed her purse and pulled Gerald out the front door, slamming it behind her.

The next day, Ramona called Gerald's home, but his wife hung up on her. Ramona called back and this time Gerald answered. As Gerald spoke to Ramona, she apologized to him for how she acted, but Gerald's wife was yelling in the background, "I never want to speak to her again the rest of my life and I don't want her calling this house again."

Now Gerald, who wanted to accept his sister's apology, was in a very uncomfortable position. His wife now hated his sister. If he ever wanted to see Ramona again, he would have to do it without his wife, who said that as far as she was concerned, her sister-in-law was dead.

Furthermore, she told Gerald that she would never again be in the same room with Ramona at any family function, and, if she found Ramona there, she would walk out.

Gerald knew that from then on, any attempt to reconcile with his sister would threaten his relationship with his wife. He loved his wife. His sister was his family, and he loved her too, but his wife and his sister would no longer be together in his life. Gerald used a popular expression to describe his family life after these incidents. It was somewhere between a rock and a hard place.

47. THE POWER OF AN EXECUTOR

The appointment of an executor is a crucial consideration in the preparation of a will, and should not be taken lightly. Your executor will be managing and distributing the assets you leave, and often will be making decisions which will have a very serious effect on the lives of your children or other beneficiaries after you have passed away.

The executor you appoint will hopefully be sensitive to the feelings of your children - conscious of their needs and their hopes and their dreams. However, if you choose an executor only for his or her skill in managing money, an executor who only cares about the "bottom line," overlooking the highly personal needs which are likely to arise in the lives of your children, your choice may prove to expose your children to years of conflict and hostility, frustration and pain, at a time when you are no longer there to help them.

The next two stories illustrate how difficult life can be for children who live under the controlling hand of an insensitive but honest executor.

STORY ONE: Ryan and Kerry and Their Home

Dad's will left everything equally to his two sons, Ryan and Kerry. They were in their early twenties when Dad passed away. Dad was divorced at the time of his death.

The major asset in his estate was the family home, which he had received as part of his divorce settlement. When Dad passed away, neither son was living at home, but both of them wanted to move back to it because it was the home where they grew up. That home represented their memories, their family, and their history.

Dad's home had been furnished with antiques and family heirlooms that meant a lot to both Ryan and Kerry as they grew up.

What frustrated the boys was Dad's appointment of his lifelong friend, Rudy, as sole executor. Rudy was a businessman who was used to dealing with the bottom line, whether it involved time or money. As executor, Rudy had the right to put the house up for sale, which is exactly what he did. Ryan and Kerry begged and pleaded with Rudy to transfer the house to them, but to no avail. They said that the house meant a lot more to them than the money. Rudy knew that, as executor, he had the power to sell the house, no matter what the boys said, and defended his decision by pointing out that the house needed expensive house repairs.

Rudy was also concerned about the state of the real estate market, which he felt was going to fall. He wanted to sell before the housing bubble burst, and explained to the boys that he was acting in their best interests in selling before it was too late. He told the boys that emotional attachment to a property is an obstacle to realizing the best price.

The boys were powerless to stop the house sale. They felt that Rudy was abusing his position as executor, and neglecting their rights as beneficiaries. They felt that Rudy was simply trying to wind up the estate in the manner which was easiest and most convenient for him. They felt that their own feelings and wishes were meaningless to Rudy.

When they wrote to Rudy to formally tell him that Dad wanted them to have the house, Rudy ignored their letter and kept on with his efforts to sell the house. However, he said that they could remove the antiques and family heirlooms if they wanted them, but that they had to do it quickly because the house would soon be sold. They felt that when Rudy made his offer to them about removing the antiques and the heirlooms, he was giving them what they were entitled to get anyway.

The boys had no way of stopping Rudy so they consulted a lawyer to find out if Rudy had the right to sell the house under Dad's will. According to the advice that they received, Dad's will gave Rudy the power to sell the house and, in fact, Rudy was within his rights as executor to do it, without their approval.

After the house sold, both Ryan and Kerry were devastated. Completely ignoring their pleas, Rudy had sold their strongest ties to their youth. This house now belonged to an absolute stranger. What made them even angrier was that Rudy had totally misread the real estate market, and that if he had listened to them, and kept the house, they would have had a house worth a lot more that what Rudy sold it for.

To sum up their feelings, they said that Rudy may have been their Dad's friend, but that did not mean that he was their friend, or that he was immune from being sued for selling the house for too low a price.

STORY TWO: Andrea's Dream

Andrea was a talented figure skater. Her parents recognized this at an early age, and began to spend some serious money on her training and skill development. By the time she was ready to graduate from high school, she had caught the eye of some very influential people in the world of figure skating, and had done very well in amateur competition.

During the summer following her high school graduation, she lost both of her parents in a plane crash. Her parents left wills, both naming her uncle, Marshall, as executor of their estates. As in our last story, he too was a businessman who only focused on the bottom line. His views came into sharp conflict with Andrea's. From Marshall's point of view, Andrea's skating was acceptable as a pleasant recreational activity, but certainly not as a profession for her.

From Andrea's point of view, her figure skating was her life. It was also what she chose as her future career.

Her parents' wills both had the same provisions, making Marshall the sole executor and the wills provided that Marshall was to hold their entire estates in trust for Andrea until she reached 30 years of age. Marshall was given absolute discretion to spend any money from the trust funds he held for her if he considered that spending this money would be for Andrea's benefit.

Marshall wanted Andrea to continue her university education, and for that there was money. For her needs on a day-to-day basis there was money. But for what Marshall called her "pipe dream" of earning a living by figure skating, there would be no money.

Andrea consulted a lawyer to find out about her rights after she received a letter from Marshall stating that he was not going to waste her parents' hard-earned money on "distant dreams." The letter went on to say that he would set her on the right path, would do for her what he felt her parents wanted, and would not allow her to squander her inheritance. The letter went on to say that he would pay for a "real future."

Andrea not only showed her lawyer this letter from Marshall, but as well, she showed him another letter from a European amateur skating association inviting her to take part in a competition in Prague. She was chosen from over 2,000 other amateur skaters. The letter from the skating association said that Andrea would have to pay for her own airfare, ground transportation, hotel, and other related expenses. To Andrea, this meant that she would be a solid step closer to her dream of one day getting to the Olympics.

She explained to her lawyer that Marshall knew about this written invitation to compete, and still he flatly refused to give her a dime.

Andrea's concern was that Marshall had control of all the money left to her by her parents, until she reached 30. By then, it would be far too late to even think of a career as a figure skater. To Andrea, her uncle held in his hands, the career she was working so hard to achieve.

She wanted to sue her uncle to force him to take money from her trust funds, so that she could get to Prague. However, her lawyer explained that the law can be complicated in situations like this. The lawyer told her that the court would be reluctant to interfere with Marshall's exercise of his discretion if the court felt that Marshall was acting reasonably, and in Andrea's best interests. The lawyer concluded that Marshall could probably make a good case that he was acting reasonably and in her best interests because he was trying to preserve her money.

Andrea was heartbroken, knowing that her chances of forcing her uncle to see her future her way were slim.

Andrea decided not to go to court, Marshall never gave her the money she needed, and with that, her dreams went up in smoke. She never got to Prague.

48. ALL MY STUFF

It is often assumed that after we die, somehow things will work themselves out. Those who feel that they do not have to use a lawyer to make a will are often of the view that the wills they make on their own are going to work satisfactorily. The following story shows how a simple, commonly used phrase, which a father put in his homemade will, meant two different things to his son and his daughter. You will see the grief that this caused after he passed away.

A caller to a radio show was livid at the treatment he was receiving from his sister. What he had to tell us went something like this.

"She harasses me, yells at me, sends me e-mail after e-mail, and now her lawyer is writing to me again. My Dad made a will, and in it is a paragraph that leaves me all of his stuff and I split the rest of his estate, with my sister. His will says it in black and white, let me read it to you: 'I leave my son Russell all my stuff.' Those were the exact words my Dad used in his will. I know exactly what it means. I'm supposed to get all of my Dad's stuff. It's so simple. Now my stupid sister hired a lawyer for Dad's estate to take it away from me!"

Our first comment was that the expression "all my stuff" has no meaning in law and is very unclear. He said, "The meaning is very clear. I get the gold and diamond rings that Dad inherited from Mom when she died. It all became his stuff when she died."

The caller was fuming that his sister was disputing his definition of Dad's use of the phrase "all my stuff." From her point of view, this phrase only included her father's tools, sports equipment, and personal possessions. According to her, Dad's personal stuff did not include the gold and diamond rings that their deceased mother had owned, and left to their father in her will. She told the caller that the gold and diamond rings were women's jewellery and could not have been intended for him. The angry caller then added, "She's a moron! She calls me an idiot but I know I'm right! She keeps harassing me with e-mails repeating that the gold and diamond rings are not Dad's stuff. She's the idiot!"

The caller was furious at his sister. He said that the phrase "all my stuff" was clear as crystal to him, and why couldn't his sister see what was so obvious? Now the caller was about to call his own lawyer into the battle. He finished his call with these words, "I'm going to win this case. I know a judge will see it my way. I hope my sister's legal fees will cost her more than all of the jewellery is worth!"

49. PAWNS OF THE GUARDIANS

Rebecca and Kevin had two children aged six and eight at the time they made their wills. They decided to name Rebecca's sister, Pamela, and her husband, Herb, as guardians of their children. Rebecca and Kevin trusted Pamela and Herb to the ends of the earth.

Less than a year after making their wills and appointing Pamela and Herb as their guardians, an accident claimed the lives of both Rebecca and Kevin. The provisions of their wills now meant that Pamela and Herb were to be the guardians of the two young children.

As devastating as the loss of their parents was for these two children, there was even more bad news in store for them.

A few months after the two children had settled in to live with Pamela and Herb, Pamela caught Herb having an extramarital affair. Now a nasty divorce was placing the children of Rebecca and Kevin right in the heat of the battle between their aunt and their uncle. Herb unexpectedly raised the stakes in his negotiations with Pamela by claiming custody of Rebecca and Kevin's children.

The fight was bitter. Pamela and Herb had no children of their own, and Pamela accused Herb of using his young niece and nephew as pawns in his battle to extort a better settlement from her. For months, the children seemed to be at risk of having to move out from their Aunt Pamela's home.

Pamela ultimately obtained custody of her niece and nephew, but the divorce was both expensive and stressful. If only Rebecca and Kevin had named Pamela in their wills as sole guardian, and had not mentioned Herb, Pamela's little niece and nephew would have been spared a great deal of the pain and suffering they had to endure. To Pamela, it was clear that if her sister Rebecca could have seen how Herb had abused her trust, and used her two young children as pawns, she would have been horrified.

50. THE GOLD LOCKET

Harriet's will appointment left a deep impression on me. She came to revise her will in order to leave her gold locket to her only granddaughter, Jordana. Harriet told me how much her husband Bernie loved Jordana. He used to spend a lot of time with her. Jordana made him laugh, and laughter did not come easy to Bernie because he had Parkinson's disease. He had a hard time speaking, and had for years been confined to a wheelchair.

After telling me this, Harriet showed me the gold locket. She had been clutching it in one hand and then the other from the moment she sat down. I could not help but notice how she was gently lacing the locket's gold chain through her fingers as she was talking to me.

Harriet went on to tell me that she had no idea that this locket existed until she found it in a box, among Bernie's papers. With this locket she found a card scrawled in Bernie's shaky script, "Happy 50th Anniversary, Harriet. I will always love you."

It was when Harriet found Bernie's card that she began to realize just how much trouble he had gone to in order to get this locket for her. She knew how Bernie could not get out of the house on his own, so Harriet imagined Bernie calling the jeweller, and in his weak, faltering voice, arranging her surprise gift to be delivered to the house. She realized how hard it must have been for Bernie to arrange for this surprise gift all on his own.

Harriet then showed me the inscription on the back of the locket: "For My Princess. 50 Years of True Love." Her next words came in a wavering voice, "Bernie never lived to give it to me. When he died, I lost the love of my life."

Harriet could not hold back her tears. She looked up at the ceiling and said, "Thank you Bernie. I love you." Then she looked at me and in a sad voice continued, "Bernie died only two days before our 50th anniversary.

He never lived to give the locket to me. It would have meant so much to him, but I know that Bernie would be so happy to know that one day, Jordana will be wearing it around her neck."

51. PICTURE THIS

Dad was an avid art collector. When he died, he left his entire estate to Mom, and she inherited many valuable pieces of art from Dad. Because of this, she decided to make a new will, which left each of her children certain works of art. Every single piece was to be distributed as fairly as possible to each of her three children, except for one portrait that hung over the fireplace. Mom felt that her children would work out among themselves how to deal with that one piece.

Mom may have assumed that her children would work that out, but it was only after she passed away that her children's true feelings about that portrait began to surface.

Shortly after Mom died, the children began to argue with one another over that portrait. Their disagreement deteriorated into a fight so hostile that lawyers became involved.

The portrait had been done by a young European artist who later became famous. As a result, this portrait became very valuable. The ironic twist to this story can be found in the subject matter of this portrait. You see, originally, Dad had commissioned that young European artist to paint a loving family portrait of Mom, Dad, and their three young children.

If Mom and Dad were able to see how their children were fighting one another over a portrait of themselves, they would never believe their own eyes. This portrait, originally commissioned as an act of love, had the end result of tearing their three children apart.

52. HOW COULD MY BROTHER STOOP SO LOW?

Chantal had a miserable time in high school because she was bullied mercilessly by Serena and her clique. Even the fact that Chantal's older brother Stefan was dating Serena did nothing to help this situation. Chantal felt like a second-class citizen, and her self-esteem was so low that she became depressed, and had to see a psychologist. Chantal's parents tried to speak to Stefan about this, to see if he could help, but he always took Serena's side, and nothing they could say to him would work. It was only after Chantal graduated from high school and was accepted at a college far away from Serena that Chantal finally felt at peace.

After she graduated from college, Chantal went to work for a large pharmaceutical company and lived at home with her parents and her brother Stefan. Stefan was still seeing Serena, but never brought her to the house. Life continued to improve for Chantal, until tragedy suddenly struck.

Both of her parents were killed in an automobile accident. Her parents left their entire estates equally between Chantal and Stefan. For about a year after that tragedy, Chantal and Stefan lived in relative peace in the family home which they inherited from their parents. Then, unexpectedly, Stefan announced to Chantal that he was going to ask Serena to marry him.

Upon hearing this, Chantal told her brother that if he ever brought that woman into their home, he better keep her out of Chantal's sight, or else there would be big trouble.

Stefan was very serious about Serena and he wanted her to move into the house with him. Stefan spoke to Chantal about working something out, and she said the only thing that would work out is if he moved out of the house. She told Stefan that he knew how miserable her life had been because of Serena. She was shocked that he could be so insensitive to a sister. He didn't seem to care that their parents would never have wanted Chantal to be hurt a second time by such a vicious woman.

Stefan ignored everything Chantal said. He told her that he loved Serena and she was going to move into the house with them no matter how Chantal felt about it. She could take it or leave it. He owned his half of the house and he was moving Serena in.

Chantal dreaded the day that she'd see Serena again. In the early afternoon of the day she so feared, Chantal saw Stefan's car pull into the driveway. She saw him open the trunk of the car and start to unload Serena's suits, dresses, shoes, a jewellery case, and a couple of lamps. Chantal stood almost frozen to the spot as she saw her brother bringing all of Serena's things from the driveway, up the stairs, to the front porch. She knew that the next thing to happen would be that he would open the front door to the house.

Chantal, shaking with rage, suddenly sprang into action. She opened the front door of the house and began to kick all of Serena's clothing and personal effects, which Stefan had just placed on the porch, onto the grass of the front lawn. Just then, Serena pulled up in her car. Looking at her possessions scattered on the grass, she started to swear at Chantal, and came running at her. Serena grabbed Chantal, turning her around, and then slammed her heavy boot into Chantal's stomach. Chantal crumpled down the stairs of her home in excruciating pain. The fall had broken her arm, and it was her compound fracture that caused Chantal to bring a criminal assault charge against Serena.

As the criminal charge wound its way through the preliminary procedures, Stefan went out of his way to make his sister's life at home as miserable as he could. The hatred between brother and sister grew day by day, especially because Serena was kept out of the house because of the restraining order against her that emanated from the criminal proceedings.

Chantal had enough. She wanted to turn her life around at this point, before depression could set in for a second time.

First, she took a step to move ahead in her career. She applied for an executive position which had become available in another pharmaceutical company. She was lucky, and was able to quickly arrange a job interview with that company. The interview went well.

The next thing Chantal did was to initiate legal proceedings against her brother to force a sale of their home. Chantal may have been furious when Stefan had attempted to move Serena into their home, but her anger paled in comparison to the temper tantrum that Stefan threw when legal papers were served on him, for the forced sale of their home. He tore through the house, grabbing every stick of furniture he could find to build a barrier dividing his half of the house from Chantal's half. The house resembled a war zone, and after one sleepless night, Chantal knew that she had to leave. She had a good friend who would share an apartment with her until Chantal's life would settle down. Chantal packed as much as she could and left to move in with her friend.

After a few weeks living with her friend in the apartment, Chantal's life began to calm down. Every few days, Chantal would drive to the old house to pick up her mail. She was relieved that Stefan had not changed the locks. She was looking for some updates from her lawyer about the legal proceedings, and a decision from the pharmaceutical company where she had her interview. It seemed to her that both the legal proceedings and the response to her application for the new executive position were each taking a lot of time.

Just as she began to feel anxious about these issues, her lawyer's secretary called her. There was a package, private, and confidential to Chantal that was couriered to her lawyer's office by her brother.

Immediately, Chantal drove to her lawyer's office. The secretary handed Chantal her brother's package, and as she read it, she knew just how low Stefan had stooped. The package contained a letter from that new pharmaceutical company, accepting her application for the position, congratulating her, and telling her to call the human resources representative Monday morning. That Monday morning was three weeks ago. Stefan had received her mail at the house, had opened it, deliberately held it, and then delivered it to her lawyer. He had added to the letter from the pharmaceutical company with thick marker printing saying, "I guess you forgot to tell the post office that you moved. By the way, a person from this company called here and I didn't give you the message. Congratulations on the job you didn't get." Chantal immediately called that human resources person, using the telephone in her lawyer's office, and was coldly told that the position had been filled.

With that disgusting betrayal by her brother, Chantal knew that she now had an enemy, and her first step in this new battle was to instruct her lawyer to start a second lawsuit against Stefan for deliberately damaging her career.

53. MOM'S PRECIOUS FURNITURE

During the 1950's, Irwin's parents hired a custom cabinetmaker to design and build a very special mahogany dining room set, made up of a large china cabinet, a dining room table, and six chairs. The china cabinet had etched crystal panes, specially designed with engraved rose petals. The cabinetmaker started off with an artist's conception, and then designed a wooden mock-up; and finally, after months of waiting, the finished dining room set was delivered.

The dining room set was his mother's pride and joy. Irwin spoke of how she would cover the table with a protective mat and two tablecloths. His mother set up a special barrier between the dining room and the rest of the house so that the family dog could not get near the dining room. Irwin remembered when his sister, who was very young at the time, accidentally ran into the dining room cabinet, rattling its crystal panes and spilling her juice. He remembered how upset his mother was when she thought that the cabinet might be damaged.

He said that as the years passed, this dining room set continued to be his mother's most prized possession. When she moved from her home to an apartment after Irwin's dad passed away, the only way to get the china cabinet into her new apartment was to hire a carpenter to remove a large window. She also hired a crew with a crane to hoist the cabinet up four stories and to pull it in through the space left by the dismantled window.

Once all the dining room furniture was in place, the carpenter put the window back in. The process was expensive but it was worth every penny to Irwin's mother. He remembers her anxiety about the move. All she cared about was that there be no damage to the dining room set. She hovered around the movers and the crane operator, until her precious pieces were placed safely into the apartment.

The dining room set was as much a fixture in her apartment as it had been in her previous home. It seemed to Irwin that if this dining room set could talk, it would have described so many of the changes in his mom's life. Irwin, his brother, and his sister all got married, grandchildren were born, and his father and uncle passed away. It was around this dining room table that the family would celebrate birthdays, and marriages, and mourn their losses.

After Irwin's mother had recovered from a serious and life-threatening illness, she called the children together and told them that she did not want anyone to fight over the dining room set after she was gone. However, each of the children said that the other two could have it.

The matter was politely dropped at that point. However, what none of the children wished to reveal to their mother, was that they had no interest whatsoever in any of this furniture.

Many more years passed and Irwin's mother continued to keep that dining room set in immaculate condition until she passed away.

After she passed away, Irwin and his siblings attempted to sell the dining room set before the apartment had to be cleared out. Neither Irwin nor his siblings wanted it. No one seemed to be interested in buying it. There seemed to be no choice but to hire someone to dismantle the china cabinet and simply clear out everything in the apartment. Within a couple of days, the workmen took over to clear everything out.

Irwin never saw the dining room set again.

Years later, Irwin was at an art show. Hung on one wall between two paintings was a framed pane of etched crystal. Looking more closely at it, he could see a rose petal engraved in what had now become artwork. Immediately, Irwin was overtaken by the memory of his mother dusting the etched crystal door of her cabinet. Now he was sure that he knew what had happened to at least part of his mother's precious furniture.

Something so special to his mother, something so embedded in his family life, had simply been taken by strangers because no one else in his family cared about it.

What was so disturbing to Irwin was that he knew his mother wanted the dining room set to be kept in the family, and that somehow, none of her children, including himself, had respected his mother's wishes.

Irwin bought that pane of etched crystal glass at that art show. Today it is one of his most prized possessions.

54. THE ELECTION, FIGHTING MY OWN CHILDREN

We attend professional development seminars several times a year. During a break in one of these seminars, a lawyer told us this interesting story.

Before starting this story, it is necessary to explain a crucial legal concept, which lawyers describe as a spousal right of election. Simply put, in some jurisdictions, the law allows a spouse to elect for a share of the deceased spouse's estate instead of accepting what the deceased spouse's will provides for. The election is most likely to occur when the surviving spouse is unhappy with what he or she is left under the will of the spouse who has died.

This right of election has an expiry date. The surviving spouse must act before this expiry date, which varies from jurisdiction to jurisdiction.

In the jurisdiction in which this story occurred, the spousal election had to be made within 6 months of the spouse's death, in order to take effect.

Now to the story. The lawyer who told this story to us said that the case he was describing stood out in his mind because after it was resolved, he received a very expensive bottle of champagne and a heartfelt "thank you" card from his client, a widow, who had been married for 55 years to her late husband.

Her late husband's will left 90% of his estate to their two children. She was to receive merely 10% of his estate.

She had no idea about this will until her husband died. She was astonished that her husband would treat her so poorly.

In all of their business dealings, it was her husband who had contact with the lawyers, accountants, and other professionals. It was only after her husband died, that she found out what his will provided for. What she read both shocked and disappointed her, but she did not know where to turn. She did not contact a lawyer about her late husband's estate for months. The lawyer telling us the story had no idea why the widow procrastinated, but went on to tell of how he became retained as her lawyer.

She was working part-time, checking coats at the lawyer's sister's wedding. At about one o'clock in the morning, as the lawyer went to get his coat, he mentioned to her, that it was late, and that it was time for her to go home. That led to a discussion between them. She seemed to be very upset. She said that she took this coat check job because she desperately needed the money. She went on to say that her husband of 55 years left her very little in his will and that her children were mean-spirited and uncaring as to her fate. The widow began to sob. The lawyer was sympathetic, and after a bit more discussion, she asked the lawyer what he thought about the fact that her husband's will only left her 10% of his estate, and that her children were insensitive to the fact that she could barely make ends meet.

It was at that point that the lawyer mentioned to this woman that she did not have to accept the provisions of her husband's will. She had the right to make an election, and after 55 years she was likely to be entitled to a lot more than 10% of his estate. However, he went on to explain that under the law, her right to elect was only good for six months from her husband's death. Immediately she did some mental calculations and found that she only had four days left to make this claim. She was ecstatic to hear this news, but was in a panic to make an immediate appointment with the lawyer. He told her to see him the next morning, and he would do the legal work to file the election on her behalf.

After the election was filed, she asked the lawyer to write to her children to tell them that she had elected against her late husband's will. The lawyer, knowing the financial desperation in which his new client found herself, was very happy to deliver her message to her children in language that her insensitive children were certain to understand.

Her election against her husband's will changed her entire relationship with her children.

The daughter who had told her mother to tighten her belt and look for a basement apartment, and her son who had told his mother that there was no way he would give up one nickel of his inheritance, were now at the receiving end of this lawyer's letter, setting out some new facts of life that they would now have to live with.

The lawyer said that he felt that justice was being fulfilled in telling the children that their mother was entitled to substantially more of their father's estate than the 10% that his will had provided for.

The lawyer's letter set in motion a series of events which unfolded over the next several months. The children retained a lawyer who offered a settlement, but it was not acceptable. Nothing was going to be acceptable to their mother now, unless it fully complied with her demands. Now she was demanding everything the law entitled her to and not one cent less. As upset as the children were, they followed their lawyer's advice and surrendered everything their mother's lawyer demanded. Their lawyer must have advised them to avoid court at all costs, because of the added expense.

The widow was delighted. She told the lawyer that she owed her financial independence to him. She said she was no longer at the mercy of her children. She called her chance meeting with the lawyer at that wedding a gift from above. She also spoke of the sadness in her victory. She was sad because her husband and her own children put her through this.

The lawyer said that when he enforced his client's rights against her bullying children, he felt that this case was a strong illustration of the reason he had gone to law school.

55. THE LETTER

Right after you finish reading the following letter, a question for you, as a reader, is to ask yourself what you think the relationship was between the recipient of this letter and the client who instructed her lawyer to send it. We can state very clearly that the letter was not written by either of us, or by any lawyer in our firm. Our ethical obligations are such that in relating this story to you, the lawyer who wrote that letter, his client, and its recipient must all remain anonymous.

LAW FIRM OF
GRAY, GREEN, & BLUE
6708 ORANGE AVENUE
MARS, U.S.A. 11112
(888) 5*5-9898

Mr. John Doe
78 Silver Knight Place
Mars, U.S.A. 11113
July 6, 200*

BY REGISTERED AND REGULAR MAIL

Re: Dawn Smith

Dear Mr. Doe:

We have been consulted by our client, Dawn Smith, who has determined that she no longer wishes to have any type of relationship with you.

Our client has asked you on numerous occasions not to visit her home and not to communicate with her, or her child. You have ignored her requests, and you have persisted in going to our client's home without being invited, even after she told you that you are no longer welcome. Your conduct is intrusive to the life of our client. Our client will no longer tolerate your conduct and she wishes you to refrain from harassing, disturbing, or even contacting her in any manner whatsoever.

We trust that you will respect our client's rights to her privacy. In the event that you persist in harassing and interfering with our client, we will seek the appropriate restraining order through the Court to control your conduct.

No further notice will be given to you. Please govern yourself accordingly.

Yours very truly,
GRAY, GREEN, & BLUE
Per:
Harold P. Blue
Attorney

You might be surprised to hear that Mr. John Doe was the father of Dawn Smith. The purpose of the lawyer's letter was to attempt to prevent John Doe from having any contact with Dawn Smith or her child, who was John Doe's grandchild.

We are often asked what would motivate a parent to cut a child out of his or her will. There is no general answer to this. However, there is usually a reason. For example, if your son or daughter had his or her lawyer send you a letter that looked anything like this one, would you give him or her a dime under your will?

Some parents may ignore insults and offensive conduct, but other parents will neither forgive nor forget conduct of that kind.

Surprisingly, we come across people like Dawn, who have acted as she did, yet years later are shocked and offended to learn that they are not in their parents' wills.

There is an expression that fits here, "What goes around, comes around."

56. WHAT A PARENT REALLY WANTS

Bella came to do her will. She told me that she was turning 75 and that her physical health was on the decline. Mentally she appeared to be very sharp.

She talked about her childhood in England and about her many careers after graduating from college. She told me that she did her own investing even when her husband was alive. She gave me very detailed information about the nature and extent of her assets.

She said that it was harder for her to get around after her bout with pneumonia, which kept her in the hospital for weeks. She needed home care until she was fully rehabilitated.

Then our discussion took a turn, and she started to talk about her two sons and her two daughters. She said that she had always loved them dearly and always would until the day she dies. She bragged about the dentist, the computer programmer, the insurance executive, and the son who ran his own business. She was so proud of them, but I sensed that somehow, she seemed to be disappointed in them. She described how, if she needed cabs for her doctor appointments, or housekeeping twice a week, or nursing care or physiotherapy, the children would always pay for her needs. For her children, money was no object. Although they gave freely of their money, what upset Bella was that they were stingy with their time. They always seemed to be busy or out of town or occupied with something whenever she wanted to be with them.

She tried to tell her children how she felt, but her words seemed to fall on four pairs of deaf ears. Just speaking of this seemed to distress her. She summed up her feelings with these words to me, "All I ask for is that in my golden years, I form some part of my children's lives; that they want me around; that they care about me. So many mothers and fathers dedicate their lives to helping their children do well. I was one of those mothers. I gave everything I had for so many years. Aside from a birthday or Mother's Day, a mother would like a simple visit from her child. She wants a kiss on the cheek, or 'Mom, I love you,' or a call at the end of the day, asking how her day went.

When you become elderly, one of your biggest fears is to fall down in your home and break a hip, lying all alone, while no one hears you and no one discovers you until after you are gone."

Bella went on to explain that although she was excluded from her children's lives, her only grandson, Thomas, was different. He took away Bella's fear of being alone. He cared about her in many ways. Bella loved when he held her hand as they watched television and home videos together. He asked her question after question about her life and her past. His visits to her were frequent and always interesting to her. She always looked forward to his telephone calls. He made her feel important and beyond being a grandson, he was a true friend.

She described Thomas as the only person standing between her and the feeling of isolation that would take over her life if not for him.

She paused at that point. Then she said that Thomas was going to be the sole executor and beneficiary named in her will.

She ended up our discussion by saying that her guess was that her children expected to inherit her estate, but the only one who deserved it was her grandson, Thomas.

With that, the legal work began. In short, even though she dearly loved her four children, and was very proud of their accomplishments, that day in my office, she cut them all out of her will - leaving the entire estate to her grandson, Thomas.

57. I HAD TO CHALLENGE HIS WILL

A man seemed to be very anxious to tell us the following story during a break in a seminar we had presented regarding avoiding inheritance battles.

He said, "I would like to tell you my story. I want to tell you just how unfair the system can be.

My uncle was married to my aunt for over 60 years. When my aunt died, my uncle was 92, and all alone.

Shortly after my aunt's funeral, my uncle told me that since I was his last living relative, he was leaving his entire estate to me. I was also to be his only executor. He gave me his lawyer's name and telephone number, and told me that I should contact his lawyer when it came time for me to deal with the estate.

A couple of weeks later, my uncle invited me for lunch at his home. At that lunch, he told me that he was not a poor man, and went into some detail about what he owned. He told me that he was never a believer in 'keeping up with the Joneses' and that is why he drove an old car and led a quiet life.

He told me that he did not like to be alone and that with his wife gone, he wanted us to be close during the years that he had left.

I was happy to be close with my uncle. He understood that I couldn't be with him all the time because I was often away on business trips. I told him that I would do the best I could, to spend as much time as possible with him, when I was in town.

Several months after my aunt passed away, I began to notice changes in his home. It looked neater than before, and some of the furniture was moved around. There were flowers in front of every mirror. I commented on how neat his house was. My uncle smiled and told me that it was thanks to Janet, his friend's daughter. She was helping him with the house, and also did some shopping for him.

Several weeks after my uncle first mentioned Janet, I happened to be visiting with him, and she dropped in. She was a very attractive woman, and it came out in my conversation with her that she had recently divorced her husband.

From that point on, it seemed to me that, whenever I was with my uncle, the subject would somehow turn to Janet. I first became concerned when my uncle told me that he had bought her a new car. I told him to be careful because people often hear of seniors being taken advantage of. He laughed, saying, 'Janet? No way.'

As time went on, my concern for my uncle deepened. He would talk of new investments that he was advised to make because Janet had friends who recommended them. He was not interested in my opinions. He said that he fully trusted her.

One day, when I called my uncle, Janet answered the phone. I learned that she had now moved in with him. My uncle said that he needed her help and companionship. He said that Janet made him happy. I reminded him that he should be careful about being taken advantage of.

Nothing I could do or say could stop the momentum that was building up. It was no longer easy for me to see my uncle without Janet being there. It took months for me to find a private moment with him. When we finally met alone, he said that he had to confess something to me. He said that Janet told him that her divorce had taken a serious emotional and financial toll on her. He said that her finances had been depleted. He wanted to be there for her, the way she had been there for him. That is why he now put his house in joint names with Janet so that when he passed away, she would own his home. Despite my questioning him about how she was there for him, he avoided the issue.

My uncle's new attitude was cause for even more concern than I had before. I never again had the opportunity to spend 'one-on-one' time with him. However, out of respect for my uncle, I was always polite to Janet.

After my uncle died, I consulted his lawyer, and arranged an appointment. At that appointment, I learned that not only did Janet get my uncle's house, but his entire estate as well. The lawyer explained that my uncle made a new will several months before he died, revoking his old will and leaving everything to Janet. She was now appointed as the only executor of his estate.

I wondered how my dear aunt would have felt if she had known that my uncle had left everything they had once owned together, to someone outside of the family. The thought that Janet had taken advantage of my uncle made me furious. I retained my own lawyer to start a lawsuit declaring that my uncle's last will was no good, and that my uncle's genuine intention had been to leave his estate to me. This went all the way to court and I lost.

Our case was based on two essential arguments. We argued that my 94-year-old uncle did not know what he was doing, and that he was not mentally capable of revoking his old will and making a new one, leaving everything to a woman who was not even related to him. But that argument failed, when Janet's lawyer happened to find the one doctor in the entire country who would come to court and say that my uncle was perfectly fine, had all of his wits about him, and was mentally sharp.

Our next argument was that even if my uncle was mentally sharp, he was still manipulated and pressured by Janet into leaving everything to her and cutting out his only next of kin. But that argument failed when Janet's lawyer showed the court a letter, supposedly written in my uncle's handwriting. That letter said that he loved her and wanted her to have everything he could give her. I think that Janet held his pen for him as he wrote it, probably threatening to put him in a nursing home if he didn't. This supposed letter of my uncle's went on to say that I didn't need his money because I could look after myself. The judge did not believe me when I said that there was no way that my uncle would ever write a letter like that. My uncle always knew that I could use all the financial help I could get.

My lawyer advised me not to appeal the case, since the judge believed Janet. He said that an appeal would throw good money after bad. I followed his advice. Janet threw me a bone, and I won't get into what she paid me, but it was not very much. My anger just won't go away and I just felt I had to tell my story to you."

We listened intently to this man. We have heard many strange tales in our travels, but his last words to us made us shake our heads in disbelief when he said, "It is really unfair that a court would allow a 94-year-old man to make a new will!" After the nephew left us and went back to his seat, we felt very strongly that his belief in his uncle's mental abilities would most likely have been very different if his uncle's will had left everything to him.

58. EIGHTEEN WAS TOO YOUNG TO INHERIT

A gentleman called into a talk show to tell us a sad story.

His sister and her husband asked him if they could name him as executor and guardian in their wills, in case anything happened to both of them. They had two young children, Jake and Carrie Ann. The caller said that he was appreciative of their trust in him, and agreed to be named as both guardian and executor in their wills.

At the time, both his sister and her husband were in their forties. The children were eleven and thirteen years of age. It came as a terrible shock to the caller, when, less than a year later, he learned of a tragic car accident which claimed the lives of both his sister and her husband.

The caller was unmarried at the time, and had a close relationship to Jake and Carrie Ann. As a result of the tragedy, he moved into his sister's home to look after his niece and nephew.

Between the value of the home and the cashing in of the life insurance, the caller was looking after a sum which amounted to over two million dollars. He invested the money so that there would be income to support college educations when the time came.

For several years, his relationship with Jake and Carrie Ann was excellent. Everything began to change after Jake turned 17. It was at that time that Jake became interested in what his parents' wills provided for. Each of the wills provided that his parents would fully inherit from one another, but when both of them died, the estate would be equally divided between Jake and Carrie Ann. The wills said that the children would get their inheritance at the age of 18.

Friction was building up as Jake's 18th birthday was approaching. He demanded to know exactly what was in his parents' estates, and what was being done with the funds. Jake told the caller that the time for his independence had arrived, and he wanted to live in the house with his sister, and no longer needed the caller to act as guardian. Jake wanted his uncle to move out of their house.

The caller attempted to reason with Jake, but Jake was so insistent that his uncle move out, that he threatened to start legal action on the day he turned 18. Jake influenced Carrie Ann, and both of them made their uncle's life as difficult as possible.

The caller had always loved and respected his deceased sister, and pleaded with Jake and Carrie Ann to think things out. Even though they were entitled to get their inheritance at 18, he offered to manage their investments for them, and to do anything for them that they needed in order to have a secure future. However, both Jake and Carrie Ann rejected his offers and demanded that he turn over all of their money the moment they were entitled to it.

The caller tried his best, but he could not fight what the wills provided for, and he left the home, after several years of looking after the children.

The caller turned over Jake's inheritance to him as soon as Jake turned 18. Up to this point, as a result of careful management, these investments had steadily increased in value. The caller was still looking after Carrie Ann's money, and learned from the financial institutions involved that Jake had cashed in all of his investments.

The caller's relationship with Carrie Ann was hostile and strained during the last two years that he looked after her money. She accused the caller of mismanaging her money. By the time Carrie Ann turned 18, the caller was more anxious than she was, to wash his hands of this estate. He turned her inheritance over to her the day she turned 18. At that time, she was involved with a man in his forties.

The caller next learned that Jake had been involved with drugs. He had destroyed an expensive car in an accident which occurred while he was drunk. He had been sued by the innocent victim of that accident and there was no insurance to back him up because of his being impaired by alcohol. As well, Jake stopped his education after high school and began a life of petty crime. He had twice been arrested for shoplifting. It looked like Jake was going to have to go bankrupt because he had squandered his inheritance and still had to face the lawsuit of the people he injured in that car accident.

Carrie Ann moved to Europe with that older man, and the caller heard from her when she asked his advice on how to deal with her brother. Jake was demanding money from her because of the fact that he was broke. She did not want to deal with him. She was coping with her own problems in Europe. Her boyfriend left her with a child and never married her. He had used her for her money. Once the money ran out, he left her. She was now a single mother with a young child of her own. Carrie Ann told the caller that she was no longer on speaking terms with her brother.

The caller said that his sister and her husband could have avoided making the children their own worst enemies. Giving them everything at age 18 ruined their lives. Their wills could have provided that Jake and Carrie Ann would get their inheritance at a later age, when they would be mature enough to manage what was left to them.

The caller ended this upsetting story with this piece of advice, "Don't think that the words in your will are only words on a page, because one day, those words may come to life."

59. DUPED BY MY CHILDREN

Sophie was an energetic, widowed grandmother, who had once owned her own home. In the old days, she loved gardening, entertaining in her home and backyard, and cooking for her family. Generally speaking, her lifestyle was independent and comfortable.

After one of Sophie's friends broke her leg from slipping on the front steps of her home, Sophie's children became insistent that Sophie move from her home to a safer environment. The children had done their own research on a popular retirement residence for seniors. It was close to where they lived, and they told Sophie that this would make visiting her more convenient. They convinced Sophie to sell her home and move into this residence.

Sophie trusted the judgment of her children, sold her home, and moved into that seniors' residence. Her decision was heavily-based on her mental image of her new life in the retirement residence. In her mind's eye, she foresaw her weeknights and weekends spent with her children and grandchildren.

Regrettably, these images turned out to be far from the reality of life in her new residence. Sophie quickly found her life there to be emotionally empty. The visits that she expected did not materialize. After her children helped her move in, she heard from them by telephone, but their visits were very brief, and far apart.

Haunted by the rich memories of the life she led in the home she had sold, Sophie began to doubt the wisdom of her move.

She sorely missed the familiar creak in the living room floor of her old home. She was nostalgic when she thought of the scents of that house, such as the pine scent from the furniture her late husband had built. She missed the sound of the young children playing in the next door backyard.

She remembered the little lines she and her husband had marked on the door post of the kitchen, to measure the heights of their children as they grew up.

Now she missed the view from her kitchen, with the trees that grew up with her children. Only a small remnant of her furniture stayed with her after the move to this retirement residence.

She knew that many of the other people in her building were happy with their lives, but for Sophie, this was turning out to be an environment that she disliked. She had little in common with the others in the building, and there were no real friends to make. She felt that she had been too quick to listen to the advice of her children. She had already given them most of the money that came in from the sale of her home, and now she had closed the door to the life that had meant so much to her.

Still, her biggest complaint was that her children had little time for her. They visited her infrequently, and all of their visits were short. Her grandchildren rarely came to see her. She never seemed to get an invitation to visit any of them in their homes, other than on special occasions. Her house was once the focal point for everyone in the family to meet; but now that it was gone, the family unit seemed to be gone as well.

Sophie consoled herself with the hope that her family would visit her more often. However, the weeks would go by, and the only footsteps she ever heard coming toward her room would continue to someone else's room. Sophie began to realize that her children had persuaded her to give up a life that meant more to her than anything else she could imagine. She seemed to be lost without her home, and she felt that her children had convinced her to do something for their own convenience and not for hers.

Sophie resigned herself to adapting to this residence, but she bitterly felt that her children had duped her into accepting life's consolation prize.

60. MY KINDNESS CAME BACK TO HAUNT ME

When Mom got sick, Olivia was the daughter who moved in to look after her. Regine was the daughter who didn't seem to care too much about Mom's predicament. Regine had her own life, with her own husband and children, and Mom's illness was not going to interrupt her routine.

Regine's attitude upset Mom. Mom confided in Olivia that Regine wouldn't even spend her money on the gas to drive over and see her. Mom said that the only time she ever seemed to hear from Regine was when Regine needed something.

For over a year, Olivia never once saw Regine at Mom's house. Olivia knew that this was upsetting to Mom. However, Olivia never imagined how angry Regine had made Mom until one day Mom said to Olivia that she was going to change her will and give her entire estate to Olivia, cutting out Regine.

When Olivia heard this, she persuaded her mother not to totally cut Regine out because Regine was still her daughter, and she should get something from the estate. As well, Olivia didn't want to face the wrath of a sister who was totally cut out. Persuading

Mom to leave something to Regine was no easy task, but in the end Mom relented and decided that Olivia would get 95% of the estate, leaving Regine to get the remaining 5%. This decision made Olivia feel good. She was pleased that she was able to convince Mom to include Regine in her will.

Olivia was at peace with these arrangements, but soon after Mom passed away, Olivia began to realize what a disastrous effect her goodwill gesture was going to have. She described what she had persuaded Mom to do as "Mom telling the burglar where to find the keys to the house."

Even though Regine was getting only 5% of Mom's estate, she exploited the fact that she was entitled to be treated the same way as anyone else with rights to a share of an estate. To Regine, this meant 5% of anything Mom left, including every single item of furniture, jewellery, and anything else in the house.

Regine made Olivia's life miserable, and badgered Olivia relentlessly in demanding an accounting and attempting to second-guess every single act carried out by Olivia as executor. Regine complained that Olivia sold the family home prematurely and got too low a price. Regine wanted compensation from Olivia personally for what Regine called a shortfall in the value. Furthermore, Regine felt that Olivia made poor investments with the estate's money. Regine said that the return on the estate investments was too low, and that again Olivia was personally indebted to her for the shortfall in investment return.

Even though Regine's claims may have been exaggerated, Olivia, as executor, still had to formally respond to those claims.

Olivia knew that she had created this situation. She was being punished for something she had urged Mom to do, out of the goodness of her heart. She tried to explain this to Regine, but Regine retorted by accusing Olivia of pressuring Mom to cut down Regine's share. Regine continued her harassment until the very last dime of the estate was distributed, and then the two sisters never again spoke to one another.

There is a valuable lesson in Olivia's story. Where a will leaves a beneficiary even 1% of an estate, that beneficiary is placed in a position where she can watch every act of the executor which might lower the value of her 1% stake. She can demand an accounting from the executor and can complain about perceived shortfalls and even possibly sue the executor for shortfalls in this 1% share. But where a will leaves a sum of money to a beneficiary, and not a percentage, the result is dramatically different. Once the executor pays that sum of money to the beneficiary, the obligation of the executor is completely fulfilled, and the beneficiary has no further interest in the estate.

61. TAKE AN INTEREST NOW

A caller to a TV call-in show had a very important message that she felt should be passed along to the television audience. She said that she married many years ago, at a time when it was common for women to let their husbands look after the family's financial affairs. She confessed that she always left it to her husband to make their investments, and never took an interest in the family's money or business. When her husband unexpectedly died, she said that she felt lost and helpless for too long. She did not know about the investments he made, and didn't even know where to look to find what her family had, or what her family owed. She could only get some limited information from her late husband's accountant.

She said that her message was not only to the women out there, but to everyone who lived together. She said it was important for both partners to take an interest in their financial affairs. Who are the business contacts, such as the lawyer, the accountant, and the life insurance agent? What are the bank passwords and the computer account passwords? Where are the bank books, the key to the safety deposit box, and the investment information?

She said that everyone out there ought to take an interest now, or else they will be forced to become an expert later, and learn the hard way, just like she had to do. She said that when her husband left this earth, he took all of the information with him, and she didn't know where to start. Her first year-and- a-half after he passed away was not only a time of mourning, but of stress and panic as well. With a tone of conviction in her voice, the woman ended her comments with these words, "Get involved. Take an interest, and open your eyes so that you will be prepared for the worst, if the worst happens."

Wise words indeed.

62. SHARING THE ARIZONA CONDO

This story might be looked upon as a heads-up to parents who are leaving real estate to their children.

Dad's will was straightforward. He loved his daughter, Claire, and his son, Tyler, and left everything he owned equally to the two of them. This included his Arizona condo. As fair and simple as this sounds, the equality provisions of his will actually caused a lot of grief to his two children after Dad passed away.

In the process of settling Dad's estate, the two children decided that they would equally own the condo and that they would share it. Between them, they agreed upon a schedule where Tyler would use the condo for his family during certain months and Claire would use it during other months.

As straightforward as these arrangements might sound, there were some serious problems under the surface, which did not take very long to emerge.

There were certain facts of life underlying these problems. Tyler was always a very neat individual, and his wife, Judy, might be described as a "neat freak." Claire, on the other hand, was never neat. As a child, she was the one who was always reprimanded for leaving her clothing and remnants of her meals all over the family home.

Claire and her family had the first stay in the condo. When Tyler and Judy took over for their first turn, Tyler's wife, Judy, could not help noticing various deficiencies that irritated her, and she made her feelings very clear to Tyler. Judy noticed that the screen door to the condo balcony was broken. The balcony needed re-tiling. There were stains on the bedroom carpeting, and the kitchen needed new flooring. She pointed out to Tyler that there was personal money which they could set aside in order to improve the condo, but it was upsetting to her when she learned that Claire had no intention of putting a dime into any improvements.

At the end of their first stay at the condo, Tyler and Judy left it sparkling clean. However, when they returned for their second stay, they found old rotting food in the fridge, crumbs on the floor, beds unmade, pots still on the kitchen counter, dirty dishes in the sink, and water in the bathroom sink that sat with a film on it because the drain to the sink was plugged. Tyler had to get a plumber and a cleaning crew to make the condo liveable for Judy and him. Judy later learned that one of the reasons for the slothful conditions she found was that Claire's daughter had hosted a party for her friends in the condo and had left it in a terrible state. Now Judy wanted Claire's daughter banned from the condo.

In fact, when it came time for their third stay, Tyler arrived a day earlier than Judy so that he could clean the condo and attempt to hide from Judy, the worst of the mess he found.

It was on the occasion of their fourth stay that Judy had had enough. When she arrived, she found that Claire had left soiled clothing on the bed, and assorted swimwear, sandals, and a tennis racquet on the living room couch. At the bottom of the closet was a pile of Claire's clothing, which should have been on hangers. The condo had the general appearance of a disaster zone.

Tyler went to the supermarket to stock up on food for their stay. By the time he returned to the condo, it looked almost habitable. He asked Judy what happened to the mess. She told him that she dumped all of it into the garbage.

When Claire subsequently learned that almost all the clothing and personal possessions which she left in the condo, were thrown into the garbage, she was furious at her sister-in-law. Claire told Tyler, "I hope your stupid wife doesn't leave a pair of shoes or anything else in the condo because next time I go there it will wind up in the garbage. How could she do this to me? Who does she think she is? I hate her!"

Tyler found himself caught between his wife and his sister, desperately trying to keep the peace. He continually had to act as a peacemaker and a buffer between Judy and his sister, Claire.

What began to really worry Tyler was that if he died before his wife, she would inherit his share of the condo from his will. That would make Judy and Claire co-owners of the condo. How would the two of them ever work out such an explosive situation?

Tyler thought of what his father's visions must have been of his two children sharing the condo: dinners together, swimming in the pool, playing cards around the kitchen table, and laughing hysterically as his children told their children the funny stories they shared while growing up. Tyler could almost bet that his father would never have dreamed that the condo would turn out to be a theatre for a war between the families of his two children.

63. THEY WEREN'T FAIR TO MY BROTHER

Christene could do no wrong in her parents' eyes. They always told her how special she was to them, and how proud they were of her. They would continually brag about her to family and friends.

On the other hand, her parents considered her brother, Steve, to be their "problem child." As far as her parents were concerned, Steve ate too much, drank too much, and smoked too much. He was lazy and he associated with people they despised. Nothing Steve did was ever good enough for them.

Christene did not see Steve in the same light as her parents saw him. She felt that they had overlooked his many good qualities. She tried to convince her parents to look beyond Steve's faults, and to see the goodness in him. However, Christene's arguments had no effect on the way her parents chose to see Steve.

First and foremost, Christene felt that Steve had always been a loyal son, even in the face of the attitude of their parents. She knew that no matter what, Steve would have always been there for them. She also looked upon Steve as a brother who would do anything for her, and she loved him for this.

It was a personal disappointment, but no surprise to Christene, that her parents decided to cut Steve out of their estates. Their wills left Christene as their sole beneficiary. She was also their sole executor.

Her father died first, leaving everything to her mother. Her mother decided to keep her will as it was, and was adamant that Steve would be disinherited.

When her mother died, Christene knew full-well of her mother's intention to cut Steve out of her will. However, Christene voluntarily gave half of what she inherited to Steve. She wanted him in her life, and she felt that leaving Steve empty-handed would spoil her relationship with him. In the end, she felt that she had to reject the wishes of her parents. She wanted to right a wrong, and that was far more important to her than to benefit financially at the expense of her brother.

64. FOUR GENERATIONS, THEN TO A STRANGER

Garrett had come to my office to prepare his will. He was in his mid-forties, never married, and had no children. Both of his parents had already passed away. He had only one sibling, his brother, Lyle. Garrett told me that he wanted to make a will which would prevent Lyle from ever benefiting from his estate.

When Garrett came to my office, he said that he wanted his estate to be left to two friends whom he had known since high school. When I asked Garrett why he was excluding his brother, Lyle, he became very upset and began to tell me of all his reasons for hating his brother and for wanting to cut him totally out of his life and his will. At that point, Garrett mentioned that besides giving his two friends his estate, he wanted to give one of them a special gift of two solid silver candlesticks. Garrett was adamant that his will contain an exact description of these candlesticks to ensure that they would go to his friend. He wanted his will to specify that if his friend died before him, the candlesticks would go to his friend's wife.

When I asked him why he was going to such lengths to ensure that his brother would not inherit those candlesticks, Garrett exclaimed, "There is no way that those candlesticks will ever get into my brother's dirty hands!" Garrett explained that the candlesticks were one of the few things brought over to this country from Ireland by his great-grandfather in late 1800's. These candlesticks had been passed down from his great-grandfather, to his grandfather, then to his father, who then left them to Garrett.

Garrett told me that Lyle had betrayed the family name by fighting over their father's estate. Garrett said that his brother had to be taught a lesson and punished for what he had done after their father died. For these reasons, he said that even if it meant breaking all ties between his family and those treasured candlesticks, he wanted to be sure that no matter what happened, his brother would never get them.

I prepared the will following Garrett's wishes. He said that he felt that signing the will was a source of relief for him. After Garrett left my office, an image came to my mind of Garrett's great-grandfather packing those candlesticks deep into his suitcase for the voyage across the ocean to North America. I thought of how his great-grandfather may have had to protect that suitcase from thieving hands. I thought of how proud Garrett's great-grandfather would have been to hand those candlesticks to his own son.

My next thought was about Garrett's high school friend, who would inherit these candlesticks one day. A stranger to the family would own two silver candlesticks, without knowing where they came from, and without knowing their history, all because of the conflict between Garrett and Lyle. It was sad to think that a fight between two brothers broke a chain of possession four generations in length.

65. A FRUGAL FATHER

Marjorie felt very deeply that money is the root of all problems, and this is the story she told us.

Her husband, Bradford, was a strict father who taught their only son, Joey, to respect the value of a dollar. During the Depression of the 1930's, his own father raised him that way, and that is how Bradford wanted to raise Joey.

Bradford had always lived within his means; and he left no stone unturned to ensure that Joey lived this way as well. Joey had to learn to live on a small, weekly allowance, and for anything more he wanted, it meant delivering newspapers, cutting grass, or shovelling snow. Bradford had no interest in giving Joey handouts so that he could keep up with his friends. In fact, Joey could not keep up with his schoolmates, and suffered with the reputation of being "the poor boy" in school. But Bradford's motto was that if Joey could not afford it, then he had to live without it.

Bradford's frugality meant that as Joey went through his teenage years, he rode an old, rusty bicycle while his friends rode new ones. He couldn't join an organized sports team with his friends because Bradford refused to pay for sporting equipment or any of the fees necessary to join a league. There were no designer labels of any kind in the home, nor were there any luxuries. In fact, Joey had to earn his own money to pay for most of his school supplies, even the ones that were needed in his classes.

Joey often complained to his mother, Marjorie that he worked hard, did well in school, and deserved better treatment from his father. He could not understand why his father was so tough on him, and why his friends were treated so much better by their parents. Marjorie felt that Bradford was too strict, but went along with him because she had no money of her own. Bradford was the breadwinner and controlled the family money. She also told Joey that parents had to act as a team. She said that she wished she could do more for him, but that he should be patient, and she was sure that things would one day take a turn for the better.

Joey listened to his mother and endured an artificial poverty dictated by his father. Despite these difficulties, Joey worked very hard and was proud that he was accepted at college. He was always good in math and science and wanted to get a degree in engineering. But Bradford would not give Joey any of the financial support he needed in order to enrol in college. Despite the fact that the family was well-off by this point in time, neither Joey nor Marjorie could persuade Bradford to give, or even loan, the money needed for Joey's college education.

Joey felt more than anger when he saw his friends go off to college while he had to give up his chance. He took a job, and shortly after that, Joey packed up his few belongings and moved out of the house.

In the working world, Joey was as diligent as he had been in high school. Before long, he began to experience financial stability for the first time in his life. But his feelings of childhood deprivation never left him, and these feelings began to turn to an anger which grew stronger as time passed. He was a loving son to Marjorie, but rarely spoke to Bradford.

As the years passed, the communications between Joey and Bradford faded to the bare minimum. Marjorie ultimately arranged a meeting between Bradford, herself, and Joey, in a "last ditch" effort to try to salvage Joey's relationship with his father. The meeting was not successful. Joey held nothing back. He blasted Bradford for forcing him to suffer through the best years of his life for no good reason. He spent his youth as a second-class citizen. He lost his chance at a college education. All he learned from Bradford was how to suffer. So now it was time to give Bradford an ultimatum.

Joey had been looking at a house to buy for himself and his young family. So if Bradford wanted a relationship with him, it was time for Bradford to reach into his pocket and show Joey that he was serious about making amends. So Joey asked Bradford for a down payment on the house he wanted to buy. Bradford refused. Now Joey's fury could not be contained. He screamed an expletive at his father and yelled, "You selfish *******! After all of this, you still haven't learned! Well you are going to learn now! You will never see my son again, and he will never, ever know you!"

As Joey stormed out, he told Marjorie that as far as he was concerned, she was his only parent.

About six months after that meeting, Bradford developed pneumonia and was hospitalized. Marjorie called Joey to let him know. She told him that Bradford's prognosis was not good. Bradford was in the hospital for weeks on end. Never once did Joey visit him, or even call. Marjorie spent most of her days in the hospital. About a month after the time that Bradford was hospitalized, Marjorie was speaking to Joey, and as they spoke, she was momentarily hopeful, then abruptly disappointed, when, within one short conversation with her son, Joey asked her, "Do you have any good news? Is Dad dead yet?"

Joey's astonishing question took Marjorie by surprise, but she regained her composure and told Joey that in fact she did have good news. Almost miraculously, Bradford began to respond to a new drug that the doctors were giving him. She was overjoyed to tell Joey that Bradford was going to recover. But there was silence at the other end of the phone. She asked Joey what the problem was. He did not answer. He did not even say "goodbye" to Marjorie. The phone just went dead.

Bradford's brush with death had awakened him to what a gift life really is. Before he got sick and entered the hospital, he had revised his will, cutting Joey out of any inheritance because of Joey's hostile attitude toward him at their last meeting. Bradford had even persuaded Marjorie to cut Joey out of her will, too.

However, now that Bradford had recovered and had returned home from the hospital, he decided that even if Joey never spoke to him again, he would part this world with his head held high. His first step was to arrange for new wills to be drawn so that Joey would once again inherit after he and Marjorie were both gone. Marjorie immediately agreed. His next step was to try to bring Joey back from his icy silence. He told Marjorie to invite Joey for supper, but she told Bradford that he must be dreaming. She told him that there was nothing he could do or say that would ever bring Joey back. "But I want to see my son!" he replied. "Bradford, you don't want to know what he said to me about you. He wants nothing to do with you. He considers you dead."

"A father is always a father," Bradford said, tears welling up in his eyes.

In all of the years that she had known her husband, this was the first time that Marjorie had ever seen him cry. Tears began streaming down his face, as they spoke.

For over an hour, Marjorie listened as her husband's emotions poured out. One moment he was agonizing over the loss of his son, the next moment he was cursing himself for being so stupid for so long. Finally, Bradford seized the moment and picked up the phone. He called Joey. Marjorie was looking at her husband as he held the telephone to his ear. The conversation lasted less than a minute and the only words that Bradford uttered were, "Hello, it's Dad." Marjorie saw Bradford's face turn pale by the time he put down the telephone. She asked him what their son had said. Bradford looked at her. His eyes seemed lifeless. He sat down on a chair and held his head in his hands. She asked him again what her son had said. He just shook his head and Marjorie then knew that Joey would never again speak to Bradford.

Bradford lived for seven more years after that. Never once, for the rest of his life, did Bradford ever get to speak to or even see either Joey or his grandson. After Bradford passed away, Marjorie told Joey that he had hurt his father badly, but Joey shrugged off her comment, saying that he felt no love for Bradford.

Marjorie then said, "You hurt Dad terribly. He went to his grave always hoping that you would come back to him. He blamed himself for hurting you. He wanted to make it up to you." With that, she showed Joey Bradford's will naming Joey as a beneficiary along with Marjorie. Joey looked at his mother coldly. "Too little, too late, Mom."

As sad as this was for Marjorie, it was only a year-and-a-half later that she would get to feel the full emotional impact of the destruction of her family unit. She was helping her young grandson, who was in grade six, with his school project. The teacher had asked the class to prepare a family tree. The boy took Marjorie by surprise when he asked her why he never met his grandfather or spoke to him. He asked her what he was like. "I wish I would have gotten to know him," the boy said. She had difficulty finding any words that could reveal the truth to her grandson. What she did say was that his grandfather loved him very much. But what she thought to herself was, "How would my grandson feel if he knew that he had missed out on a relationship with his grandfather because of one thing - money."

66. THANK YOU, DAD

After his mother passed away, Carey lived in the family home with his father. Their relationship was somewhat less than perfect, but it was hard for Carey to move out on his own. Carey was irritated by the fact that his father never seemed to find a way to praise him. What made this even worse was the fact that his father always seemed to be bragging about Carey's only brother, who had a successful career, was already married, and was raising his family in his own home.

Carey, on the other hand, never found a girl who could meet with his father's approval. Every girl he ever introduced to his father brought out negative comments. As well, his father ridiculed Carey's spending habits, and constantly accused him of "letting every dollar he had slip through his fingers."

Eventually, Carey met a girl named Miranda and he fell in love with her. When Carey introduced Miranda to his father, his father seemed to accept her. A few months later, though, after showing his father the expensive ring which Carey bought for Miranda, his father accused him of spending money on her like water. This led to many arguments between father and son, over money.

The most inflammatory part of Carey's relationship with his father was that every month, Carey's father demanded that Carey pay rent to live in their home. His father's insistence on this rent money pushed father and son even further apart. More than once, Carey tried to reason with his father. He told him that none of his friends had to pay rent to stay in their homes, but no amount of arguing could change his father's mind.

The choice put to Carey was simple. Either pay the rent or move out. There was no way that Carey could afford to move to an apartment in the right location, and his father knew it. His father's home was close to Miranda and to his work. As a result, Carey consistently paid what his father asked him to. Carey felt that his father's greed had spoiled their relationship and Carey's anger boiled inside him.

Carey was still living in the family home when his father died. Carey's father had never shown him his will or even spoke of it. After the funeral, Carey found his father's will. The will left Carey the family home, plus a large investment account worth tens of thousands of dollars. The balance of the estate was divided equally between Carey and his brother.

The generosity of his father's will astounded Carey. What surprised him even more, however, was a letter that his father left in an envelope, with the will. His father's letter said that all of the rent payments Carey had made to him were deposited into the investment account he left for Carey, and that the account also held the interest on all of the money. His father's letter said that now Carey would have a nest egg for when he decided to get married. The letter also said that it hurt him to force Carey to make the rent payments, but because of these rent payments, Carey now had money that he would never have had if he had not been forced to pay the rent every month.

It dawned on Carey that his father never wanted to benefit at all from the rent payments. Everything his father forced on him was for Carey's own good.

After realizing everything his father had done for him, Carey regretted all of his bitterness, and the anger he had felt towards his father. He wished he could take back all of the angry words he had ever uttered to his father - but now, it was just too late.

67. SOME SANITY

We were guests on a show in which practically every caller had a story to tell about vicious, hostile fights between various family members. There seemed to be no let-up to the negativity that was flowing that evening. There was a change in the mood of the show close to the end, when a lady called in to say that she was very upset to be hearing all the stories of families being torn apart over inheritance disputes. She said that the only reason for her call was to bring a little sanity into a show filled with so much insanity.

She couldn't understand all of the greed and the hatred over things that she felt were only temporary possessions. She said that she hoped that all of the people in the listening audience would pay attention to her words, which she wrote down after her mother died. She asked us if she could read what she had written down. These were the words that she read over the radio.

"It is not Mom's pearls that I want. It is her pearls of wisdom that I miss. It is not her ring that I want. It is the ring of her telephone call to say goodnight to me that I miss. It is not her house that I want. It is her home filled with love, and the laughter of my Mom and Dad, and their hugs and kisses that I miss."

As we listened to her read those tender words, we were so touched by them. At the end of her call, we thanked her and said to her that one day, when we had the opportunity, we would pass along her wisdom to others. In attempting to fulfil our promise to her, we are now passing along her words to you.

68. HE WAS A MULTI-MILLIONAIRE

For thirty years, Len ran his service station for ten hours a day, six days a week. His hands and nails were blackened by the oil and engine grease that were part of his everyday life. For the last twenty of those thirty years, he had been my client.

One day, as he was just finishing off a car on the hoist when a gentleman in a business suit arrived, unannounced, and asked for a moment of his time. Wiping some grease off his hands, Len motioned to the gentleman to sit down, and apologized for not shaking his hand.

The man in the business suit represented a large, commercial real estate developer who wanted to buy the property that Len's service station was on. And, they were willing to pay some serious money for it.

Len had owned the property for years. He was in his mid-sixties, and was getting tired of his daily routine. He said that he would sell for the right price. The man in the business suit told Len that he would have a written offer within a week.

Len's excited call came to me when that offer was delivered to him. He had to see me right away.

I looked at the offer. It was straightforward and uncomplicated. There were no conditions. The purchase price was for seven million dollars. It was scheduled for a sixty day closing. All Len had to do was sign and he was sixty days away from being a multi-millionaire.

Len was very happy with the price. As a result, Len signed the offer exactly as it was, and sixty days later, I closed the deal for Len. When I handed Len his bank draft for the purchase money, I could see in his eyes that he was just now beginning to take in the reality of millions of dollars in his hands, and he became very emotional. It was at that moment that Len began to tell me what this money meant to him. He would never have to wake up at four in the morning again to get ready to go to work. No more would he be breathing engine exhaust, nor would he be looking with envy at people wearing business suits, their hands and nails clean. He said to me, "Now I'm a multi-millionaire, and I will live the rest of my life like a king."

I felt euphoria when I handed Len the bank draft that made him so emotional. I knew that his life was about to change.

There is no question that this was a dramatic and uplifting event. I felt the afterglow for weeks, and this feeling made every day seem to be just a bit more pleasant for me. I just could not stop feeling a sense of euphoria over this change in Len's life. I knew that he had worked so hard for so long, and now his ship had finally come in.

My mood was shattered several weeks later, when Len's son unexpectedly called to tell me that his Dad had a massive heart attack and died. With that call, I suddenly became the lawyer for Len's estate only weeks after serving as his lawyer for his new fortune. Now I had to deal with the estate of a man who was not only a client, but a friend. He had known such happiness only weeks ago. Within a mercilessly short time, I had shared in both the ecstasy of Len's property sale and now the tragedy of his death.

69. PROTECTING A BEST FRIEND

A woman called in on a talk show and said that she wanted to talk about how the special wording in her will was designed to protect her best friend in the world. She said that all of the calls on the show that she heard so far were about protecting family members. She said that sometimes, love is not just reserved for your own kin. She then told us a touching story.

Life had dealt her many unfair blows. She had undergone a painful miscarriage. Then prayer and patience seemed to reward her with a baby boy who brought joy to her and her husband. The lady sobbed at this point as she explained how, after a number of happy years, she then lost both her husband and her son.

She said that after suffering these tragedies, she felt like the loneliest person in the world.

What next came into her life was Charlie, who brought constant sunshine to her. He never left her side. He never complained. Now that her eyesight was weakened, she relied on Charlie more than ever. She told of one incident when she was about to step into traffic, and would have been hit, if not for his growl. Yes, Charlie was her beloved dog.

You could hear her love for Charlie in her voice. She felt that he would outlive her and needed someone to look after him. She spoke about how good she felt because she left money in her will to a young girl who would look after and love Charlie. She touched us, and probably the listening audience, when she said that she looked upon Charlie as her own child. She spoke of being at peace knowing that after she passed away, Charlie's home was going to be with someone who would love him like she did.

They say that a dog can be a man's best friend. In Charlie's case, we believe that his owner's foresight, in the way she structured her will to accommodate him, showed that dogs can have best friends, too.

70. A STORY OF LOVE

Three months after the death of her husband, Lorne, Charlotte came to my office, wishing to revise her will.

Charlotte was in tears as she told me that she would never meet anyone who could fill the shoes of her late husband. "Lorne was one-of-a-kind. He was so wonderful." She then asked me if I would mind if she spoke to me a little bit more about Lorne. I encouraged her to speak, and she thanked me, saying that just being able to share her feelings would help to console her. What she then had to tell me has stayed with me.

She spoke of lean times in the late sixties, when she and Lorne, who were then in their early twenties, got married. Lorne did not have steady employment, and the young couple moved in with Charlotte's parents.

Even back to the time they were dating, Charlotte's father had wanted her to find "a better match," and he didn't respect Charlotte's husband-to-be. Her father felt that Lorne would never be able to make a living.

From the very outset of the marriage, Charlotte's father called Lorne a bum, whom he ridiculed and embarrassed in front of her and in front of the entire family. Charlotte could only guess at what transpired behind her back, when her father spoke to her siblings about Lorne. Her father would often ask her why she couldn't find a decent person to marry, like her siblings did.

But despite this humiliation and mistreatment, Lorne never talked back to Charlotte's father and never showed him any disrespect.

Her father's constant criticism had inspired Lorne to open up a shoe store, and to make something of his life. As time went on, Charlotte and Lorne continued to live with her parents in their home. When Charlotte's mother became very sick, Charlotte became her caregiver. Charlotte devoted almost her entire life to looking after her mother. Lorne never complained. He was not a strong man, but he would always somehow find the strength to carry Charlotte's mother into the car from the wheelchair. He would carry her up and down the stairs in the house because there was no washroom on the main floor. He would do the maintenance and repairs on the house. He would shovel the snow in the winter and do the gardening in the spring and summer. It was because of Lorne that Charlotte's mother was able to live at home instead of being institutionalized.

Charlotte and Lorne raised their two children in that same household, and taught their two children to love their grandparents. Charlotte called this "a house of three generations" because her parents and her children were living together with Charlotte and her husband.

When Charlotte's father developed a heart condition and was forced to retire, Lorne would take him to his hospital and doctor appointments. When Charlotte's father became hospitalized, Lorne would often close his shoe store early so that he could keep Charlotte's father company in the hospital.

When Charlotte's father recovered from his illness, Lorne would spend time with him, and take him to baseball games, and he talked at length with him. They became close friends. Her father came to realize the quality of the man Charlotte had married. One day, her father called Charlotte and Lorne together privately to tell them that he was going to change his will in order to add an extra gift of money for Lorne. Lorne said "no" because what he did for the family was out of love and he did not want any money for it.

It was then that Charlotte's father made a heartfelt apology to both of them. He said that words could not express how very sorry he was for making all the humiliating and insulting remarks about Lorne to Charlotte and her siblings that he had made in past years. He told Charlotte that she had married a gem.

At the funeral of her late father, it was Lorne who gave a eulogy that brought the entire congregation to tears.

In the course of sharing this story with me, Charlotte was sobbing almost constantly. It was Charlotte's way of bringing forth her memories of Lorne, the man she loved so much. Her last comment was, "This is what it means to be in love. My father was right. Lorne was a gem."

There are endless stories of people who are unhappy in their marriages. Words like "divorce," "separation," "lawsuit," and "court" are commonplace. What made this story so memorable was the love between Charlotte and Lorne, which survived a life made more difficult by financial stress and family illness. Only death could pull Charlotte and Lorne apart.

71. IN ANNA'S NAME

One of the more touching will appointments I can recall, involved an elderly widow named Krystyna. She never had children of her own, yet wished to leave her entire estate to a particular charity which helped children displaced by war or disaster. She told me that she had done very extensive research on this charity, so that she would be absolutely certain that after she had died, all of her estate would be used to help children in need.

Since she never had her own children, I was curious as to why she had selected this charity. "Because of Anna," she replied. I must have appeared puzzled to Krystyna when she answered me that way because then she went into a longer explanation.

Krystyna told me that Anna had been her very best and closest friend when they were young. They lived next door to each other in a village in Poland. She said that she saw Anna every single day, and Anna was like a sister to her. Krystyna's eyes began to tear up as she then described an image that would stay with her the rest of her life. That image was Anna screaming, "Krystyna, Krystyna, help me, help me!" as Anna and her parents were being led away by the Nazis. Krystyna then looked at me, and asked, "What can a little girl do when soldiers with guns take away her best friend and her family? I was just a little girl. I was helpless."

Sadly, Krystyna never saw or heard from Anna again. Krystyna described how she had lived with Anna's memory ever since the 1940's. She told me that each time there was a knock on the door, or even a ringing of the telephone, she would wonder if it was her friend, Anna. But no matter who came to the door, or who called her, it was never Anna, nor was it anyone who had any knowledge of Anna. She also told me of the nightmares that came to her so many times over the many years that passed since that time.

Krystyna looked at me in silence for a few minutes and the only words she said were, "I was so helpless when she and her family needed me most."

She was evidently re-living that horrible moment, and broke into tears as she added, "The only way I can ease my pain is to leave my estate to the right charity. By doing that I can at least pay tribute to Anna's memory by helping other children. I could not help Anna then, but I can help other children in need now."

72. A REAL HERO IN MY OFFICE

Stanley had just lost his wife and contacted me to make a new will. He was an elderly gentleman who spoke with a British accent. I recall that he walked with a limp and that he wore a patch over one eye. We conversed a bit as he gave his instructions to me, and I formed the impression that he was a down-to-earth individual.

It was several months after Stanley signed his will in my office that he passed away. I met his children for the first time when they contacted me about his estate. During the course of our discussion, they began to fill in details of Stanley's life.

They wanted me to know about their father before going into the financial aspects of his estate. I will try to use the words of Stanley's eldest son, who spoke for all of the children, in order to do justice to the depth of their respect for their father.

"Dad was always shy and reserved, and I am sure that he never told you about what he had done for others during his life. Dad was a true hero. He received a medal for saving the life of a fellow soldier. The reason he lost his eye was that he took a bullet in order to save another soldier's life. The limp came from shrapnel that was forever embedded in his leg. This occurred when he was almost killed in a mortar attack."

Stanley's son showed me a picture of his father being hugged by a woman in war-torn Europe. As he pointed to the picture, the son proudly said, "Our Dad had saved her son from being shot by the Nazis."

There were other war stories. Then he told me of events after the Second World War.

"My Dad studied engineering, and he dedicated his life to developing products, such as wheelchair controls, that would help disabled people. He would travel to faraway places to help young children and other war victims."

There were also stories of how he was a hero to the family. "When Mom had a stroke, he never seemed to leave her side, yet always had time for all of us."

After hearing what Stanley's eldest son had to say, I told him that his father had not mentioned a single word of any of this when he had met with me. The children replied that their father never told anyone, except for the family. They said that he did not do what he did in order to brag about it, but he did it because it was the right thing to do.

Their parting words were that not only had they lost this wonderful man, but that the world had lost him as well.

After they left my office, it began to sink in that I had met with a true hero, and that he had been in this very office. He had been sitting right there in that chair giving me directions about what to do with his estate.

The appointments that I had had with Stanley were strictly business. I didn't know him beyond the fact that I was assisting him with his will. It was very different the day I met Stanley's children. That meeting was mostly personal.

As I sat there, I had an overwhelming desire to have had just one more meeting with Stanley. In that meeting I would have expressed to him my feelings of respect and appreciation for what he had done so unselfishly for others. Although I knew that this meeting with Stanley could never happen, I was so glad to have learned from his children what a hero their father was.

73. WORDS OF WISDOM

In our world, we not only meet people from all walks of life, but we often meet them at a time when they look back on their lives in a way that is different from their ordinary day-to-day routine. Sometimes they speak of their mistakes, sometimes they speak of their successes. In all of these cases, we listen, and try to distil wisdom from what they have chosen to share with us. Here are examples of some of those words of wisdom.

WORDS OF WISDOM A. A client once told us, "If you are going to own a car repair shop, you better know how to fix a car yourself."

He knew from experience what it meant to be dependent on an employee who could hold you hostage.

Years ago, our client lost his car repair business when the mechanic who worked for him gave him an ultimatum, quit, and could not be replaced. The repair shop was known as the place to go because of the quality of the work that the mechanic performed. Our client was excellent as a public relations person, and he was a very good manager. Unfortunately, he himself could not do much more with a car than to fix a flat tire.

After that, our client, an accomplished chef, started a restaurant business, something he could run with his own two hands. He did hire an excellent chef, but if the chef were to quit on him, he could take over completely on his own, for as long as it might take until he would find the chef's replacement. Our client was not only successful, but was also much happier, knowing that he would not be held hostage again.

WORDS OF WISDOM B. Another client, who was a successful mass marketer, said, "Think like the people, not like the king. There are a lot more people than there are kings."

WORDS OF WISDOM C. From another successful businessman: "Opportunity doesn't always knock. Sometimes you have to make it knock." He laughs when someone calls him an "overnight sensation" because to this businessman, "overnight" really means 20 years of knocking on doors trying to make things happen, that would not have happened by themselves.

In all of the 20 years, this same businessman was in business, he only had two employees who ever quit. Everyone else stayed because, in his words, "I treated them like family. When my business prospered, they would prosper with it. They knew they could come to me with their problems and I would give them a compassionate ear. They knew that I cared for them as people and not just as employees."

WORDS OF WISDOM D. Les's late Mother left him the following wisdom. She wondered why people fought over rugs, rings, and trinkets when the greatest treasures were not in their safety deposit boxes. She knew that the most beautiful assets of their family were the family members themselves. She also felt that parents should help their children financially when the children really needed the help. Children should not be made to wait until after the parent dies. The way she put this was that she wanted to give to her children "with a warm hand and not with a cold one."

WORDS OF WISDOM E. A client of ours looked many years younger than his 95 years. We asked him what his secret was. His words made a lasting impression upon us.

He told us this: "My way of looking at life is to count my life in summers. I lived to appreciate each of my summers because, as each one passed, I knew it would be gone forever. The older I became, the more precious each summer was to me. The way a 20-year-old thinks of the years he or she has left is very different from the way a 90-year-old thinks. When I was 50, I knew I would be very lucky to have 40 summers left. When I was 70, I felt that if I had ten more summers that would be a blessing. Now, every summer to me is a gift.   So I have come to appreciate everything in my life just the same way as I appreciate my summers."

The words of this elderly gentleman have helped us to realize just how short life really is, how fast it goes, and how important it is to make the most of every day.

74. TALKING TO YOUR PARENTS ABOUT WILLS

We were guests on a radio show. The main topic of that show concerned the difficulty that seemed to confront adult children in speaking to their parents about estate planning. There were two questions put to the listening public:

1. "Would you feel embarrassed about asking your mother or father if they had a will?"

2. "If you ever did have a discussion with your parents about this or a similar subject, how did you initiate it, and were you happy or upset that you did?"

Some of the answers that we heard were interesting and worth repeating here.

One caller said that his parents had initiated a discussion involving all four children. The caller said that nothing was problematic with anyone until his parents asked the children what they should do with the family cottage.

Every point of view expressed by the children seemed to meet with an objection from someone else. These were the initial suggestions:

*The cottage would be left equally in the parents' wills to all four siblings;

* The parents' wills should leave the cottage to one child and compensate the other children with gifts of money;

* The estate would sell the cottage to the child who is the highest bidder. This would be paid out of the inheritance of the child who wins the auction; and

*The caller's view was that the parents should give the cottage to all four children now, while the parents are still alive. This way, the parents would be there to iron out any disputes, and the parents would pay any taxes and legal fees involved in the transfer.

The caller went on to repeat that there were arguments over all of these proposals. No one seemed to agree with anyone else.

After his parents heard all of the shouting and arguing at this meeting, they decided that there was only one way to solve the problem. They lost no time in calling their real estate agent to put the cottage up for sale.

Another caller also had three siblings. These were his comments.

He and his siblings first met in the absence of their parents. They decided among themselves that the caller would "break the ice" with Mom and Dad, and tell them that the children wished to have a serious discussion with them about their wills.

When Mom and Dad agreed to have this discussion, all four children were there to ask whatever they wished. It was understood that nothing would be held back, and the issues that came out included the following.

*Who owed money to Mom or Dad and how much and when was it to be repaid?

*What gifts did Mom or Dad give to each of the children? How much money was involved? Was it clear that these were gifts and would never have to be repaid by the sibling who received that gift?

*What was the "real" financial position of each of the siblings? What did each of them really have? (The point here was that if one of them had a large home but it was heavily mortgaged, or a luxury car that was leased, no one should form the impression that the sibling who had a good lifestyle was wealthier than he or she really was. This would avoid the temptation to think that the sibling with the high lifestyle wouldn't need his or her inheritance).

*What personal items would each of the siblings want from their parents' personal possessions or furnishings?

*Would Mom and Dad make up-to-date wills naming executors acceptable to all four children, and up-to-date powers of attorney naming attorneys acceptable to all four children?

After explaining how this family discussion removed a cloud that had been hanging over all of the children, and how delighted he and his siblings were with the results, the caller added one more thing. He said that while the children had raised many questions to ask Mom and Dad, they had only one question to ask their children: "How come you kids waited so long to do this?"

Another caller was a parent who had something to say to all of the listeners who might be inheriting from their parents. She agreed that communication between the generations was important; but her advice to those in the younger generation was not to push their parents, and not to be overly demanding.

She said that children should know where to draw the line, and what it means to prod too deeply into the affairs and the lives of their parents. She said she had two adult children from her first marriage. After her first husband died, she married her present husband.

When her two children raised the issue of her will, she felt that they were insensitive to three things.

First of all, they put pressure upon her to make them the only beneficiaries of her estate. Their approach was to think of themselves as the object of her estate planning, and they forgot that she and her husband still had a life to lead together.

Secondly, they forgot that the money they were so worried about was money earned by the years of work and sweat of their mother, and that they did not lift a finger to earn any of this money.

Finally, they failed to respect that over twenty years ago, she had fallen in love with, and married, the man who was now her husband. She said that she would not pass away without protecting the man she had decided to spend the rest of her life with. She said, "He is my husband, not my roommate!"

The disrespectful and pressuring attitude of her children made it clear to her that her two children failed to recognize what was so personally important to her. As a result, all of the estate planning talk came to an immediate and grinding halt.

She ended by saying that while she still has her wits about her, she would make all of the decisions about where her hard-earned money would go after she died. She said that after her failed attempts to talk with them about her will, she decided that she would not allow any input from any of her children about this.

Another caller said that his family was the "Ostrich Family." He said that everyone's head was in the sand when it came to talking about his mother's will. Neither his mother, nor anyone else, would talk about money, or what she owned, or where it was supposed to go after she died. Now, two years after his mother died, her estate was still being fought over. Lawyers were involved, not only because there were disputes among his brothers and sisters, but also because there were questions about what belonged to the estate. He finished by saying, "My family paid a hefty price for not talking when we had the chance."

The next caller had a happier story to tell. She was one of three daughters. At one point, she and her sisters asked their mother whether she had a will. Their mother said that she would make sure that she would leave all three of her children protected. And true to her word, she left her girls with a solution that worked for her estate. The caller said the money was divided equally, but aside from money, which is easily divided, her mother left many antiques, items of jewellery, crystal, china, figurines, silver, valuable paintings, and household items. These all had to be divided among her three girls. Her will referred to a handwritten letter, which contained the formula that solved the problem of distributing all of these items.

The caller said that she was happy to share her mother's formula with the listeners, because it worked so well for her.

1. First, each daughter would privately select ten items from the household, and list these ten items on a piece of paper.

2. No one would know what the others chose until the three sheets of paper were placed on a table side by side.

3. Where an item was chosen by one girl and not by any of her sisters, that item would belong to the girl who chose it.

4. Where an item was chosen by two girls, and not by the third, the two girls would flip a coin for that item.

5. Where an item was chosen by all three girls, no one would have it until they would bid on it. The highest bidder would take that item.

After the first thirty items were dealt with, they started over with a second set of ten for each to choose, and kept going until everything in the house was distributed.

She said that her mom's formula worked for her family, and that she didn't want to keep it a secret.

The next call seemed to put everything into perspective. The caller was one of three siblings. The caller and his two sisters agreed with their father about how they were going to deal with his household items after he passed away. It would normally sound unusual for children to divide up everything that belonged to their widowed father while he was alive and well. However, in this caller's situation, their father wanted them to do all of the choosing while he was alive, so that he would be able to settle any disputes that might arise. The arrangements were that he would keep everything they chose anyway, for as long as he lived. All that would happen would be that every item chosen would have a sticker on it with the name of the child who would get it after their father passed away.

The choosing, according to the caller, did not go very smoothly. The process took from about two o'clock on a Sunday afternoon to about midnight. During this lengthy process there were negotiations, trading, bartering, and, as well, there were arguments, insults, and accusations among the three children. More than once, their father had to step in to smooth out the process. Finally, after this ordeal, the three siblings shook hands, and each of them left their father's home, exhausted but relieved that all of this was behind them for once and for all.

Six months later, due to an electrical short circuit, his father's house burned to the ground, along with everything in it. Thankfully, his father was rescued unharmed. The caller said that he and his siblings knew that a message had been sent to all of them.

75. IF ONLY I GET A SECOND CHANCE

Joshua, a man in his late thirties, had been diagnosed with a condition that required brain surgery. His surgeon told him that the procedure was very risky. If it was successful, his life would come back to normal; but if it failed, he might become mentally incapacitated, and worse yet, he might not survive the operation. In view of the opinion of his surgeon, Joshua asked for an urgent appointment to give me instructions to prepare his will and his power of attorney documents.

When I met Joshua for the first time, he was extremely nervous and I can sum up our meeting as one involving the organization of the affairs of a person who expected to die.

Several days later, Joshua came back to my office to sign his will and his power of attorney documents. He said that he would be operated on in 48 hours, and that he was seriously worried that he might not make it.

I remember that he was quiet as the documents were being signed and witnessed. Once they were signed, though, he looked up at me and asked, "Is that it?" I nodded my head, at which point, Joshua became very emotional, and what he had to tell me will stay with me for the rest of my life.

He told me that he was a hard-working man and that his wife understood the demands of his profession. He told me about his friends who went to Florida to escape the winter for weeks and months at a time, and that he was too busy to take off time like that.

He said that his professional life dominated his personal life. He said that in his working life, there was no such thing as a clock when it came to ending the workday. He spoke of some nights when he got only four hours sleep and some months where he never took even one day off.

He went on to say that he had a family that deserved more from him than just the money he brought into the household. He said that he was too insensitive to the birthdays of his wife and children, and that he never had time to celebrate properly.

He said that the family vacations were always on the agenda for next year, but next year never seemed to be the right time. Now he realized that there might never be a next year for him.

Joshua said that when he was younger, life seemed to be infinite, as if he had hundreds of years to live out his hopes and dreams.

Now, in his mind, all that was left to Joshua was 48 hours. What would he give now to be able to go to his daughter's dance recital next week?

He said that if only somehow he survived this operation, he would be a changed man. His family would be his number one priority. The first thing he would do if he survived would be to buy a pair of plane tickets to the Bahamas and spend a couple of weeks with his wife in the most luxurious hotel he could find. After that, he would make a point of always coming home early and watching TV with his daughter and his son, and share all the laughs with them that he could.

Then Joshua looked at me, and said that it was time to go. He pulled a lottery ticket out of his pocket and gave it to me. He said that he probably had as much chance of getting through his operation in one piece as I had of winning with that lottery ticket.

The day after the operation, I called Joshua's wife to see if everything turned out all right. She told me that Joshua's operation was a success and that his doctor expected him to have a full recovery.

I called Joshua about two weeks later. He asked me if the lottery ticket he gave me was a winner. I said, "No." He answered, "Well, I was a winner. My doctor said that I will be okay. Now, I'm going to live the life I told you I'd live. My wife and I bought tickets for a wonderful trip, and I'm going to keep my promises, just as I told you when I was in your office."

76. THE HEALTH SCARE

Rick inherited a medium-sized manufacturing company from his father. After his father passed away, Rick became the chief executive officer. He felt that his father had treated the employees too leniently when he ran the business. Rick was determined that nothing would stand in the way of profitability, and that he would operate the company his own way. That being the case, he ran the company with a very tight grip.

Short-tempered and demanding, Rick was a man who commanded respect and instilled fear among his employees. Rick expected everyone who worked for him to do whatever had to be done to carry out his agenda. He hated all surprises, good or bad. To Rick, a surprise meant something out of his control, and he had to be in control, at all times.

He once fired a temporary secretary for a typographical error. On another occasion, he embarrassed an employee in front of others for being five minutes late for a meeting. She broke down in tears. Rick was aware of the shortcomings of his personality, but if his temper and his use of power worked for him, he was not going to change his ways.

Rick ate properly and kept fit with regular exercise; but one day, shortly after his 50th birthday, he needed an answer to a strange new feeling of fatigue that was bothering him. He was also concerned about his loss of appetite. He felt that he was starting to lose weight that he never intended to lose. From what he had heard about symptoms such as these affecting men about his age, Rick began to panic, thinking that he might have a serious disease. Immediately, he made an appointment to see his doctor, who arranged for him to have a physical examination and to have his blood tested.

Rick had fallen into the grip of an overwhelming fear. He could not shake the feeling that life, as he had known it, was about to change for the worse. As he walked out of the lab where they took his blood sample, his mind could only focus on getting the results of those blood tests.

That night, he had dinner with some friends who spoke of their concerns about a stock in which they had each invested heavily. Their discussion was not important to him. He just could not tear his mind away from his health worries.

Everything seemed trivial now; the only things that mattered to Rick were the results of those blood tests. The suspense was unbearable. Rick was used to snapping his fingers and getting immediate results. Two days passed after his blood tests, with no word from his doctor. Rick was in an agonized state of mind. The two days seemed like a month. He felt a jolt of anxiety with every telephone call that was put through to him thinking that the call was from the doctor.

Rick began to prepare himself for some bad news.

If the news really turned out to be bad, he wondered whether he would still be able to maintain his leadership in front of his employees. Considering how harshly he treated them, would any of them show any compassion for him? Would the rest of his life now consist of visits to hospitals, doctors, and medical labs for tests and surgical procedures? These worries flooded his mind and washed away almost everything else that had been of concern only a few days earlier.

The third day after the lab test was a Friday. After another miserable morning, Rick went out for lunch to at least clear his head. He returned to his desk to find a pink message slip that contained the words "call your doctor." He knew it came from his secretary. He questioned her. "Who called? What did they say? Did they sound worried?" The secretary knew none of the answers to these questions. It was just a message. He remembered staring at the message slip. He dreaded making that call to his doctor. Yet he had to dial the doctor's number to end the torment. He reached the doctor's receptionist. He asked her if the results were in. She said that they were available but that the doctor was gone for the weekend. She told Rick that the doctor would be in the office on Monday and that she could make an appointment for him to discuss the lab results Monday morning at eleven.

Rick remembered the suspense overwhelming him at this point. He tried to decipher the tone of the receptionist's voice. Was she shielding him from bad news? Did she even know what those results were? All he could do was to beg her to make an exception for him, and he asked if she could please leave a message at the doctor's home to ask if the doctor could just call him. She told him she was sorry but that was impossible.

Rick spent a sleepless and tortuous weekend. He recalls driving by a hospital over the weekend, imagining patients with tubes in them, being wheeled around in wheelchairs, thinking that in only a matter of weeks, this could be him. He remembered the wobbly feeling that worked its way from his stomach to his bowels and then to his thighs. He remembered his hands shaking.

It was finally eleven o'clock Monday morning, and the doctor did not keep Rick waiting long. "Rick," said the doctor, "I have good news for you." The rest of what the doctor had to say was just a blur. The doctor spoke of some medicine he was prescribing for Rick to make his problem go away. Impulsively Rick hugged the doctor. It was at that moment, that Rick realized exactly what was important in life.

77. HER FOOTPRINTS

When we meet with a client to do a will, we are meeting face-to-face with a living person who is giving instructions to us. It is very different, however, when we are appointed as executors for the estate of a person whom we have never met. We are, to some extent, being asked to piece together the financial life of a person who had been a stranger to us.

To give you an example as to what we get to see when we become involved in this sort of estate as executors, let us describe the appearance of the home of an unmarried woman who passed away when she was in her mid-sixties. She had been an active, working woman. She had no husband, no children, and no near next of kin. She had a sudden and unexpected heart attack.

After her funeral, I opened the door to her home and walked into her last hours, frozen in time. Her kitchen was decently organized. In her refrigerator was an unopened carton of fresh orange juice. A piece of meat for her supper had been taken out of the freezer and was on a dish on the counter, completely defrosted, and now inedible.

On her kitchen table she had left a grocery list and a memo to make a phone call. Beside the memo were some supermarket coupons. A dishtowel was neatly draped over the middle of her double sink. There was a bookmark in the book she was reading. She had photographs mixed in with her business papers. It occurred to me that those photographs meant enough to her to be preserved among these papers. On the other hand, without her, and without an immediate family, those photographs showed her with people who would forever remain anonymous to me. There was no one I could possibly even contact, who could find any meaning in those pictures. I remember looking intently at some of those photographs. I remember feeling that if I looked hard enough, somehow I could raise some meaning from them.

There was a picture of her holding hands with a soldier in uniform. There was a palm tree in the background. But there was no reference in anything in her paperwork to a man. I wondered if they were in love, and where that ended up. She was never married, but why? Was he killed in some faraway war? Was she heartbroken? Did this prevent her from meeting another man? In the end, it was all a mystery. Yes, she had these pictures; but now, they had no further place to go. There was no longer any home for them.

I happened to be in her house, but too late to be part of her life. I was simply part of the footprint she left on this world. As her executor, I had to unravel parts of her life that were intimate, even secret - parts of her life that she would have hardly exposed to the world at large. What had been a life as we all recognize it, was now a shadow, made up of documents and bank records, furniture, and dishes. Years of a life dictated by her working world, now boiled down to the investment documents, bank statements, and tax returns, which I neatly arranged on her dining room table, side by side.

I still cannot escape the feeling that what all of us are doing right now, at this very moment in time, can't be that different from what she was doing during her working life. We work, spend, invest, worry, do our best to manage our money, our debts, and our calendars, and try to save for a rainy day. When I was in her house, looking at her things, this overwhelming thought moved over me like a fog that suddenly engulfed the room. I thought, "I am taking care of her business now that she is gone. One day there will be someone taking care of my final business when I am gone."

All of this brings back the words engraved on a very old headstone that I had seen while walking by a cemetery. These words were evidently addressed to all who passed by this grave: "I was once like you. One day you will be just like me."

78. IT HAPPENED SO FAST

Sometimes, a person just never recovers from a broken heart.

A young man, who had just turned 30, came in for an appointment concerning his will. He became emotional as he told me that he had an inoperable brain tumour. As we began to discuss how his estate was to be distributed, I became, in a sense, a shoulder for him to lean on. He began to pour out details about his life. He told me he was single and how close he once was to marrying the love of his life, a girl he met in college. He described her as his soul-mate and the only one for him. The heartbreak he endured when she broke off this relationship was indescribable, and merely speaking of it drove this young man to tears.

He said that when you are told that you have less than a year to live, you realize that you will never form another relationship with a woman. He felt that he would never know what it would be like to be married, or to have his own family. He also told me of how close he was to his mother, to whom he was leaving his entire estate. He did not know how to tell her that he was running out of time, and that she would most likely outlive him. He said that his mother would be devastated if she knew the truth.

A week after this sombre meeting, the young man returned to sign the will. This time, the meeting was businesslike, without any mention of the emotional matters that had dominated our previous session together.

Since this man was now so different at this meeting, I actually convinced myself that things might not turn out to be as bad as it seemed in our first meeting. I began to think that the story he told me, which moved me so deeply, could somehow end less tragically than to have this young man leave this earth at such a young age.

As he took his will away with him, I remember a feeling of optimism. Not for a moment did he speak of death. He left with a warm handshake and a smile.

A few weeks later, I was following my morning routine which includes my reading of the daily newspaper. Like most people, I decide what I will read first by looking at the headlines. However, the day's headlines were not what caught my attention. Instead, I saw a familiar face – a photo in the obituary section. It was the same young man who had come to my office. I stared at the photo in total disbelief. I thought to myself how eerie it was that he died so quickly after we met.

As I sat there with my neglected cup of coffee getting cold, I looked out the window. The sun was beginning to light up everything outside. I had so many questions that would never be answered about this young man. Who wrote the mournful poem under his picture? I reasoned that it was probably the person whom he had said was his closest companion – his mother. I also wondered if his college sweetheart would see this obituary. How would she feel? Would she experience regret over a long-lost love? Then I wondered if she had ever really known how much she meant to him and how he considered her to be the love of his life.

79. THANKING A TRUE FRIEND

My secretary told me that my next appointment would be with Samuel, who was unable to come into the office, and who I would have to see in his truck, in our parking lot. When he made the will appointment, he had told her that he was physically disabled because of the stroke he had suffered the year before.

The first time I saw Samuel was in the passenger seat of that truck. His shirt was torn and soiled and he looked like he had not shaved in a long time. He introduced me to his friend, Roger, who was sitting behind the wheel.

Then Roger said, "Look, I know you need your privacy, so I'm going to go for a coffee and I'll come back in half an hour. Come on in to the driver's seat, and I'll turn on the air for you…it's hot enough out there." With that, Roger started up the truck. He turned on the air, raised the windows, left the driver's door ajar, and walked out of our parking lot. He then turned the corner and disappeared from my sight.

I got into the seat he left for me behind the wheel, and I looked at Samuel, my yellow-lined notepad in my lap, having no idea what I would hear.

"Allow me to introduce myself, sir," he said. Samuel began to explain that life had been hard for him since he had left high school, and that life became even harder for him after his stroke. There were few people who had earned his trust in the fifty odd years that had somehow managed to slip through his fingers. But Roger was more to Samuel than flesh and blood. Roger had been there for Samuel forever, since early in high school. Roger was there when Samuel's first wife left him, and Roger was there when Samuel's second wife died. Roger took the fall for Samuel and served time in jail for him when Samuel got suckered into a bar fight.

Samuel continued, "Look, Mister, I worked hard for years, never spent much, but never needed much. My mother left me something, but I'm not a rich man. But I'm a proud man. After my stroke, Roger took me into his home, and that is where I'll be until the end of my road."

As Samuel unfolded his story, there was no doubt in my mind that he was of sound mind, and it was clear that he knew that the end was in sight for him.

He told me that anything he owned would go to Roger. It seemed to me that if Samuel could have found a way to leave his very heart and soul to Roger, he would have. Samuel's parting words to me that day were to the effect that he couldn't pass in peace until he knew that Roger would have all of his worldly possessions, such as they were.

I excused myself, and asked my secretary to go out to Roger's truck to set up an appointment for the next week. The will would be signed and witnessed in the truck. Roger would have to excuse himself once again, for a second time.

On schedule, Samuel signed the will the very next week. He told me that he wanted me to keep the original will in our office.

Here's a word, though, about the gratitude of Samuel. Before I left the truck, he grasped my hand, his eyes moist, and handed a folded white envelope to me, and simply said, "Thank you." He sat there, looking at me with those moist eyes, as I closed the driver's door.

That was the last time I ever saw Samuel. The envelope he had handed me contained a bank draft for my fees and a note expressing his thanks for seeing him in the truck, and for giving him my time.

Samuel passed away the following spring. I found out when Roger called to tell me. Other than knowing that he was the executor, he could only guess as to what was in the will. Roger told me that he wanted to do whatever needed to be done to fulfil his friend's last wishes. Roger knew of one bank that Samuel dealt with because, from time to time, Roger would drive him there to save his friend the taxi fare. From Roger's comments, it appeared that there would be little, if any, legal work to be done for this estate. In fact, Roger said that he wanted his friend to die with a good name, and, if there were any debts that Samuel left, Roger would pay them personally.

I made an appointment with Roger to come in to pick up the original will. This would be a quick ten minutes so that Roger would know that he was named as executor and sole heir to whatever it was that Samuel owned.

Roger came in and brought the death certificate, pension papers, and a funeral bill. There was nothing much for me to do, so I handed him the original will, keeping a copy for my file, and that would be the end of it...but not quite.

The next day, I got a call from Roger. He found a bank book and a small envelope with some keys in it. They appeared to be safety deposit box keys. Roger asked me if I would be available to help him with the bank, if he needed assistance. I said that I would gladly help him with whatever it was that he needed.

Later that day, Roger called again. This time he did need help, because there were going to be some complications with the bank. He had just lost his friend, and the last thing Roger needed was to get into scrapping over paperwork on whatever it was that Samuel had left to remember him by. Could I possibly then, take the time to meet with Roger and the banker? Roger said he would pay my fee. He said he just wanted to get this business over with.

We set up the bank appointment for the following week. Roger would come to my office to pick me up, and we would drive there together.

As we drove to the bank in his van, Roger did not say very much. He did repeat what he had said before though, about wanting his friend to leave this earth with a good name.

At the bank, we met with a young lady who assured Roger that there would be no problem using the few hundred dollars left in Samuel's bank account to help him pay off the funeral bill. Roger showed her the three keys from the envelope that Samuel had left him. There was a tag on each one of them with a number. She asked us to wait in her office so that she could see if those numbers matched their safety deposit box records. A few minutes later, she returned. She asked for the original of Samuel's will. Roger gave it to her and she returned again a few minutes later. She handed the will back to Roger, and said that yes, the keys matched their records, and the signature on Samuel's will matched as well, and that all three boxes were still in Samuel's name. "Would we like to see them?" she asked us.

I was very curious as to why Samuel would have not only one, but three safety deposit boxes.

The young lady at the bank asked us to wait a couple of minutes more in a private room while she got a trolley for the boxes. She then wheeled the trolley out to the private room where Roger and I were waiting. We took the first box from the trolley to put on the table. It was heavy. Roger asked me to open it to see what was inside.

It was packed solidly with bars of gold. The second box was a lighter one. It had stock certificates in a neat pile clipped together with a thick paperclip. As well there were large brown envelopes containing gold coins from South Africa and various other countries.

There was a note saying that these were from his mother's estate. There were silver ingots. There were gold rings. The third box was similar to the first one, crammed with gold bars. In this box was a handwritten note, signed by Samuel and addressed to Roger. I handed the note to Roger. He was speechless. He motioned to me that I should read the note to him. By its date, I could see that the note was written more than three years ago. The wording of that note went like this.

"Dear Roger: You stuck by me in the darkest part of my life. You never asked for anything from me. You were not just my only friend. You were more than a brother to me. I'm leaving you everything I own. When I leave this world, I will leave it in peace because I know that I will brighten your life."

Roger was almost too overwhelmed to talk. As he looked at the letter I handed back to him, tears came to his eyes. He managed to say that he didn't expect anything from Samuel. Whatever he did, he did, because his best friend needed his help.

As I reflect on this client and his friend, Roger, I cannot help but be impressed with the fact that Roger was prepared to pay for his friend's final expenses. In the end, Roger never did have to put his hand in his pocket to keep the name of his friend in good standing. In fact, when Roger retained me to help him to settle the estate Samuel had left him, we now had to deal with an estate worth almost a million dollars.

80. CAN YOU EVER FORGIVE YOUR SIBLING?

From time to time, we give seminars to the public on the subject of wills and estates. In a typical seminar, we will speak for about an hour, and then invite questions.

One seminar stands out in our experience as the longest and most emotional one we had ever given. It was not the agenda, nor what we had to say, which created such intensity, but rather one question posed to us by a woman who attended our seminar. Let us refer to her as Jennifer. Her question was one that we had never been asked before. The issues raised by her question drew out the emotions of almost every person in that room, and probably left as indelible an impression on them as it did on us.

She asked us the following question.

"From your experience as wills lawyers, do you think that a person can separate the business side of her relationship with her brother from the personal side?"

The question was a novel and very interesting one.

When we asked Jennifer for some clarification, she said that from her own personal point of view, she was able to separate her business relationship with her brother from her personal relationship with him. She went on to say that many of the people she had spoken to on this point felt differently, telling her that they thought she was wrong to make that separation.

She then told the following story, which we now wish to share with you.

After Jennifer's father passed away, his will left his estate equally between herself and her brother. Her father's estate included the family business, which her brother had been operating for years. Her father's will gave Jennifer one-half of that business. She felt that because her brother was managing the business, and she had nothing to with it, he would at some point offer to buy her out. She felt that if or when this took place, the process would be routine and friendly. Nothing had prepared her for the way in which her brother bought out her share.

There was no discussion with her brother on this point, not even a telephone call. There was no negotiation. All Jennifer ever got from her brother was a formal demand from his lawyer, to accept his very low payout for all of her interest in the business. The letter from the lawyer continued with an ultimatum and a threat. If she did not accept this offer within a week, her brother would start another business and walk away from this one, leaving her to figure out how to get any money at all out of what was left.

Jennifer had no choice but to retain her own lawyer. The buyout did not go smoothly. She could not believe her brother could treat her this way. He was forcing her into a legal world that was unfamiliar and unwelcome to her. She could not understand his attitude because she never had a fight with him before. At this point, she said that her brother had turned into "a money-hungry monster."

Jennifer suffered constant, unrelenting stress, which affected her job, strained her marriage, and shortened her temper. The legal battle imposed on her cost her thousands of dollars in legal fees which she felt never should have been spent. In the end, she submitted to her brother's demands, and the buyout was completed without a court fight. However, what followed were many cold, silent years between Jennifer and her brother.

The silence continued until her brother lost his wife. Jennifer became aware that her brother was in great pain as he mourned his loss, and this touched a nerve in her, which reminded her of how life was when she was a young girl. It was then that Jennifer began to awaken to the fact that he was still her only brother. They had shared the same family secrets, had been raised in the same home by the same parents, and as young children, they had watched the same TV programs together while they had waited for their father to come home for dinner.

Jennifer's attitude toward her brother softened, and she called her brother to give him her condolences. He seemed to appreciate her call.

A few months later, Jennifer received a call from her brother with more bad news. He had now been diagnosed with a debilitating and degenerative terminal illness, and would have to sell his house to go to a long-term care facility.

It was at this point that Jennifer spoke to her brother from her heart. She told him that he was her brother, and that he would need all the help he could get. Since he did not have children, Jennifer said that she could not bear the thought of his having to spend what little time he had left in solitude.

Jennifer was now adamant that she would take her brother into her own home. Her husband resisted her, reminding her of how shabbily her brother had treated her during the buyout of the family business. She would hear none of that. Her husband backed down. Her brother moved into her home.

Jennifer said that caring for her brother in her own home brought back some of the warmth that she had felt when they had lived together as children. During the first months when he was under her care, the topic of the buyout, the lawyers, or their fight, was never raised. For her, it was a sore point, and she felt it was a sore point for him as well.

However, it began to dawn on Jennifer that she might never get to know why her brother had turned on her the way he did. Her need to know the answer to this question became more compelling as his physical condition began to seriously deteriorate. She realized that the day would soon come when his ability to talk or to write would fail altogether. If she could not get the answer to the question weighing so heavily on her heart while her brother was still able to talk or write, she would lose the opportunity forever.

One afternoon, as she was feeding her brother at his bedside, he said, "I know that you want to talk about what we went through." He said that he knew she wanted to talk of the bad times they had. She replied, "How could you? How could you have hurt me the way you did? You tore my life apart. I would have done anything for you. All you had to do was ask. Instead, you ambushed me, took advantage of me when I trusted you, got me involved with lawyers and expenses, and you treated me worse than you would treat a stranger."

At this point, as Jennifer was telling her story to everyone at the seminar, she was in tears. The entire room was silent, as everyone waited for her to regain her composure.

She went on with her brother's response, "It was only business. Nothing personal. We may have fought, but that did not mean I stopped loving you. We may have fought, but to me, we always had our scraps, even as kids. Just because we might have had a fight does not mean that we don't love one another. We have too much depth in our relationship to let one fight tear it all apart. I always knew you'd get over it."

Jennifer then went on to describe to us how, at that moment, they just looked into each other's eyes. For what appeared to her to be the longest time, not a word was spoken between brother and sister.

Her brother finally broke the silence with words that Jennifer said she would take with her to her grave.

"Now I know the pain I caused you, Jennifer. Forgive me. And in case I don't ever have another chance to tell you again, thank you for sharing the last part of my life with me. I love you."

Jennifer leaned over and kissed his forehead. "I forgive you."

He passed away exactly one week later.

There was silence in the room for several minutes. Then Jennifer continued.

"People might call you a fool when your brother, who treated you like an enemy and almost turned your life upside down, gets your forgiveness when he gets sick, and you take him into your home. Almost everyone who I have ever told this to said that my brother took advantage of me, and that I was wrong to let him do this. I need to know the answer." She turned around to the others in the room, some of whom had tears in their eyes, and she asked them, "Do you think I was a fool?"

We had never experienced such an emotionally intense atmosphere in any seminar we had ever been involved with. It seemed as if every person in that room was ready to say something. It was evident that in order to handle this situation properly, order had to be established immediately. We expressed compassion, but then set forth the rules. Everyone would have a chance to say what he or she wanted to say, but it would have to be strictly by a show of hands, just the same way as it had been from the start of this seminar.

Immediate control was essential because several animated conversations had already started between various people in the room. However, our orderly format thankfully prevailed from this point on.

Jennifer had raised a question that happened to hit a nerve among all who were present. It is by no means an exaggeration to tell you that more than twenty participants spoke their minds for almost three hours. However, we will restrict our comments to only a few of the more interesting points of view.

One of the first people to respond was a gentleman who described his own battles with his brother. He ridiculed any suggestion that you could ever separate the business side from the personal relationship with your sibling. He described at length how he suffered, at the hands of his own brother, who, according to his narrative, had lied, cheated, misled, and bullied his way to the lion's share of their mother's estate. He said that very many years had passed since the estate had been dealt with, but his anger never disappeared. Even to this day he described a bitter silence not only between brothers, but as well between their families. He finished his comments by saying how no one who did what his brother had done could ever be forgiven. He turned to Jennifer, and asked her, "If the roles were reversed, do you think that your brother would have taken you into his home and looked after you the way you looked after him? Would he have forgiven you? I'll bet that if he had his chance, even if you were sick, he would have drained you for every cent you ever had."

This gentleman's comments brought a wave of applause from many in the audience.

Several others spoke, basically along the same lines as this gentleman.

However, after awhile a woman stood up with a dissenting point of view. She spoke of how her mother became terminally ill. She was her mother's caregiver. She described the enormous burden she carried. Her only sister escaped this, and lived a life that was far

BARRY M. FISH & LES KOTZER

more carefree than her own. Years of bitterness resulted because she felt that her sacrifices were taken for granted by her sister.

However, the woman agreed with Jennifer, that family was family. This woman's point of view was that you had to separate the personal side from the business side, and to do your best to forgive and move on with life.

She said that she "buried the hatchet" and made peace with her sister for this reason. But she also said that there was something missing from the relationship she had with her sister, and that not all of the damage to the relationship could be repaired. She said that the pain of those difficult years flashes back when she drives by the hospital where her mother spent her final months, or when a song comes on the radio that had played in the background during the many hours that she had spent with her ailing mother. She said that she had never been able find the words to express her pain until she heard Jennifer speak tonight.

Before sitting down, she said she recognized that her own issues had arisen over caregiving and not over money. She still felt that her emotions would have been the same had this been an attempt to resolve a fight over money.

Right after that woman spoke, another woman said that it is impossible to separate the business side from the relationship side. She described a fight with her sister over a necklace that her mother had promised to her. She said that she defines her relationship with her sister as being one thing "before the day my sister ripped off Mom's necklace" and being something else altogether "after the day my sister ripped off Mom's necklace." The lady spoke of how her sister had grabbed the necklace from her mother's home right before Mom's funeral so that the speaker would not get her hands on the necklace. While her sister was helping herself to the necklace, the speaker was coming from the airport on the way to her mother's funeral.

There were many more points of view, some saying that Jennifer did the right thing by forgiving her brother, and most saying that Jennifer was really taken advantage of.

One gentleman made an interesting comment to the effect that he blamed the father who had owned the business that caused such difficulties between the brother and the sister. He said sometimes you have to blame the parents for leaving the mess. He turned to Jennifer and asked her if her father had ever even bothered to discuss what should happen with the business he built up, after he was gone. Jennifer responded that there was never a discussion on this subject. So the man concluded that, sometimes, the parents must take the blame, and it is not always the fault of the children.

One woman, the mother of four children, said that the children should know that their parents want them to get along, and that it is completely disrespectful to those who passed away, for the children to squabble over what was left for them to share. After all, the ones who passed away acquired and built up what was left in the estate, and whoever benefits is getting for free, what others have taken a lot of trouble and hard work to leave to them. She told Jennifer that she completely agrees with how she forgave her brother, and that Jennifer's father would have been very proud of her for helping her brother and for forgiving him. The woman closed her comments by reminding Jennifer that both she and her brother were her father's children. "He must have loved both of you," she said, "and he would have wanted you to love each other."

There were many more speakers, and the hour was very late. It finally came to a point where we had to call for only one more speaker. The comment of this last speaker also happened to hit a nerve with us. Coincidentally, it turned out to be very appropriate that the evening's entire dialogue end with what this man had to say.

"Maybe I am not the right person to speak on this subject. I am not yet married, and never had the good fortune to have a brother or sister. Since I was a little boy, I was envious of my friends who had brothers and sisters. For years, it was my dream that my parents would have another child so that I could have a little brother or sister.

Every single one of you who spoke here tonight had one thing in common, no matter which side of the question you were supporting. Life gave every single one of you a treasure that somehow was never given to me. You all grew up with a little brother, a little sister, or a big brother, or a big sister, to walk to school with, or to play sports with, or to spend summers with, or to go on trips with, and to share secrets with. Some of you were even luckier and were one of three or even four kids. And after hearing how some of you have squandered the treasure you were given, and have failed to appreciate the incredible gift you were given, I just can't believe my ears. My mother is very sick, and I am her only child, and everything is on my shoulders. I have to make all of her decisions for her, and I have no one to help me. I don't wish my predicament on any of you. If I had a brother or sister to be there with me, I would be glad to share everything with them, and if it came down to something bad happening, I would do anything in the world to save our relationship."

We thanked everyone for what they had to say, and our parting words were heartfelt. "We came here so that we could help you learn something about the law; but as it turned out, you helped us learn something about life."

This story is not quite over. As we were going to the parking lot, Jennifer came up to us to apologize for raising such emotion and for keeping us so late. We said it was not a question of apologizing at all, and we were indebted to her for making this evening a life experience for us and for everyone. She responded, "I didn't want to say anything in front of the audience, but there is an ironic end to my story. You see, all of my brother's fighting was for nothing. He died without a will and I am his closest living heir. I inherited everything he owned, including all of the shares he had in Dad's company. This was the company that he took away from me in the first place."

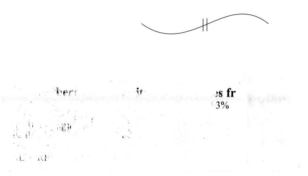

"After all, life is really simple; we ourselves create the circumstances that complicate it." (Unknown Source)